all whom god has joined

All Whom God Has Joined

Resources for Clergy and Same-Gender Loving Couples

Leanne McCall Tigert · Maren C. Tirabassi

Foreword

The Right Reverend V. Gene Robinson

THE PILGRIM PRESS · CLEVELAND

In honor of our respective life partners,

EMILY GEOGHEGAN and DONALD TIRABASSI,
co-authors in our covenants of love

The Pilgrim Press, 700 Prospect Avenue, Cleveland, Ohio 44115
thepilgrimpress.com

Printed in the United States of America on acid-free paper

17 16 15 14 6 5 4 3

Library of Congress Cataloging-in-Publication Data

Tigert, Leanne McCall, 1957–
All whom God has joined : resources for clergy and same-gender loving couples / Leanne McCall Tigert, Maren C. Tirabassi ; foreword V. Gene Robinson.
p. cm.
ISBN 978-0-8298-1838-3 (alk. paper)
1. Same-sex marriage—Religious aspects—United Church of Christ. I. Tirabassi, Maren C. II. Title.
BX9886.T54 2010
264'.05834099—dc22 2010002560

Contents

PART III · SO YOU WANT TO GET MARRIED? UNIONED? DOMESTICALLY PARTNERED?

FOREWORD

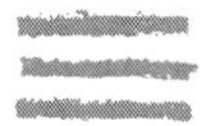

Two prehistoric tribes are gathered in front of a cave, huddled around a roaring bonfire. The two tribes eye each other with a little suspicion and a lot of hope. They have been brought together, unusually, because one of the young men has met a young woman from the other tribe while fetching water at a spring. They have fallen hopelessly in love. And while each tribe is nervous about their prospects for the future, they have come together to finalize the action that will create a new family.

Just to make sure, the father of the young woman wants to hear one last time that the young man's intentions are good and pure. Before giving up their prized young woman, the tribe wants to make sure that she will be well cared for. Even the young man's tribe is nervous for him and his future. Is she really going to be the right partner for their beloved son? Life is "nasty, brutish, and short," and he will need a helpmate. Should they trust her? Will she serve this new family well?

The time arrives. The good intentions are reaffirmed. Each tribe presents its beloved child to be joined to the other. They hear the promises each makes to the other. More than a few tears are shed. Each tribe sets aside its apprehensions, and once the ceremony is over, joins the other in celebrating this new union, and the party goes on into the night.

I have no idea whether or not anything like this ever occurred in prehistoric times. But something like it did. And something like it has continued to this day. For a long time now, we have called it marriage. Customs and practices related to this action have changed dramatically over time; marriage has evolved in countless ways. But it has endured.

Every time I sit with a couple in premarital counseling, I suggest to them that what they are about to experience is very old indeed. Oh, some of the customs have changed, it's a lot more expensive, and people are apt to come from greater distances. But what will happen at their wedding will essentially be reminiscent of what happened in nearly prehistoric times, when two tribes gathered by a fire outside a cave, each to offer one of their own in the making of a new family. Each tribe essentially looking out for its own, suspicious of the intentions of the other; each tribe with nerves on end and emotions near the surface; each tribe hopeful and joyful, wondering in their hearts if time and the fates will be good to this new family-in-the-making. Modern-day weddings, albeit with a few more flowers, matching tuxedos, and lots of chafing dishes, are pretty much the same mix of emotions—both caution and hope, anxiety and joy.

Now, with the flowering of marriage justice and equality in state after state, with many more surely to come, prior to a national resolution of this issue, same-gender loving couples are being invited into this old and rich tradition of celebration and commitment. Whether joined in non-legal religious celebrations of commitment and blessing, legal civil unions, or legal marriage, same-gender couples are seeking ways to make public the commitments they have made to one another in private and seek their community's support in the keeping of those commitments.

Twenty years ago, most leaders in the movement for equal rights for gay, lesbian, bisexual, transgender, queer, and questioning people steered clear of the institution of marriage. It was thought to be too big a mountain to climb, too much to hope for. Strategists argued that the fight for equality in the civil right to marriage was too dangerous in its possibilities for backlash from the heterosexual community and religious institutions. Evan Wolfson, executive director of the national Freedom to Marry Coalition, was virtually the only national LGBTQ leader arguing that anything less than full marriage equality was second class citizenship. Now, twenty years later, marriage equality is not only on the lips of nearly everyone (pro or con), but is a reality in many states, with more certain to follow.

This changed marital landscape brings new challenges to our religious communities and the clergy who serve them. Whether gay and lesbian couples are coming to their churches and synagogues for a religious blessing of their relationship or the solemnization of a civil union or marriage, both the clergy who serve as their pastors and the religious communities that surround and support them are having to find new ways, new words, and new rituals to celebrate this new reality.

In some ways, we are stumbling around in our support of this new reality, not unlike the early days of people coming out. Mistakes, sometimes embarrassing and often quite funny, are made as we find our way along, trying to be good companions to our LGBTQ brothers and sisters as we navigate this new territory with them. Now, help has arrived in the experience, advice, and counsel of Leanne Tigert and Maren Tirabassi in *All Whom God Has Joined.*

For much too long, marriage has had patriarchal underpinnings. For much of that time, marriage was a legal transfer of property (the woman) from one man (the father) to another (the husband). The father places the hand of the bride into the hand of the groom in many weddings to this very day. The bride has often been the pawn of economic wrangling for power and position. The answer to "what's love got to do with it?" has often been "nothing!"

Yet in more recent times, with the growing acknowledgment of women's equal personhood and rights, love has had a lot more to do with it. Consent of both parties is a historically recent development. A prospective groom's visit to the father's house to ask for his daughter's hand is now only a romantic, nostalgic throwback to the past—sweet and respectful, but hardly necessary in a time when the father's answer is virtually irrelevant to the couple's moving forward with their union.

Still, the almost primeval actions of a marriage continue to be the same: two "tribes," offering one of their own, to be joined in the making of a new family, accompanied by pledges of support and the offering of gifts, well-wishes and celebration.

Now, in our time, gay and lesbian couples seek to participate in this ancient rite. This is not just about equal rights—it's about equal rites. As gay and lesbian people have emerged from the closet, we are naming not only our reality as being affectionally drawn to people of the same gender, but also wanting to celebrate our relationships and have our families acknowledged by the larger community. Part of the respect that gay and lesbian people seek is the affirmation of our loving relationships—not just from our secular communities, but from our communities of faith.

Putting together our faith and our sexuality has been one of the most elusive of goals for us as gay, lesbian, bisexual, and transgender people. For too long, our religious communities have told us we are deviants, intrinsically flawed, and an abomination before God. For too long, we have believed them. But a new day has dawned, and a fresh look has been taken at the "texts of terror" that occur in Holy Scripture, which have been used to support those condemnations of our love. Understanding those proscriptions in the contexts in which they were authored has led us to believe that, in fact, the Holy Scriptures (both ancient Hebrew and early Christian) do not address the question we are asking today about faithful, monogamous, lifelong intentioned relationships between people of the same gender. The notion that some small percentage of humankind would be naturally drawn to people of the same, not the opposite, gender, was totally unknown in the ancient world. Even though homosexual *behavior* has existed throughout time and been variously celebrated, condoned, and condemned, sexual *orientation* is a modern construct. Indeed, such a notion, as a psychological construct, could only be posited late in the nineteenth century. The ancient world was no more able to comprehend "sexual orientation" than they would have comprehended electricity. It was simply outside their ken.

But a quiet (and sometimes not so quiet) revolution has been underway across America. In countless homes across the land, men and women have come home to say, "Mom, Dad, I'm gay." The family's understanding of itself and the parameters of its love have been thrown into chaos, while the family discerns whether or not its love is broad enough, deep enough, expansive enough, to include their gay child. In increasing numbers, in some of the most surprising circumstances, the family's eventual response has been "Yes, we can and do love our child." And in increasing numbers, families are realizing, despite their initial discomfort, that they can come to love the person their child loves. America has changed irrevocably.

This sea change has occurred just as often in families who are religious. Christians, Jews, Muslims, and people of all faiths have been challenged to take another look at the scriptures that have caused their rejection of homosexual people, once they know one of their beloved children to be homosexual. Every faith and every denomination is caught up in this debate, no matter how clear the denomination is about its rejection of gay love. This debate is as strong in Roman Catholic, Orthodox Jewish, and fundamentalist families as it is in families of mainstream, "liberal" Protestants and Jews. And in the end, for most families, love for their children trumps any ideological or theological stance previously held.

But because all this is new, because we are still finding our way in how to accommodate this new evolution of marriage, committed couples of the same gender (and the clergy who serve them) are searching for the appropriate ways to mark liturgically these new unions. Some faith communities are ready to call it "marriage" and pattern their rites after the more traditional marriage service. Still more are seeking ways to strip traditional rites of marriage of their patriarchal, property-oriented rituals, seeking rites that stress the equality and mutuality we aspire to in relationships. Still others are not quite ready to call it marriage, but are seeking to find a way to affirm and bless these unions.

Enter *All Whom God Has Joined: Resources for Clergy and Same-Gender Loving Couples* by Leanne Tigert and Maren Tirabassi. This new book, by seasoned pastors, offers a treasure trove of ideas, thinking, and suggestions about how to celebrate these new relationships with meaning, symbol, and thoughtful action. Anyone looking to construct a ceremony of union that will express her or his deep commitment to another will find this book both comforting and supportive, as well as practical and helpful. This book is jam packed with questions that should be considered in approaching and planning for such a rite of commitment. Options are suggested and explored. This is not a "one size fits all" approach, but rather a series of considerations that will walk a couple through all those things they might do and say to make the rite of union their own unique expression of their love and commitment to one another.

It is high time for such a book, and I am delighted to commend it—not only to those considering such a ceremony, but to those who counsel them. Clergy—even gay and lesbian clergy—are generally unused to helping prepare a same-gender couple for such a ceremony, and while there will be similarities to traditional marriage rites, there will also be special considerations for gay or lesbian couples.

Pastoral issues will abound surrounding such a service—not the least of which are the couple's feelings in response to a parent's or sibling's potential refusal to attend or participate due to their religious objections to the union. This is different from a parent who doesn't like a particular mate chosen by their child for marriage, because the rejection here goes to the heart of who these two people *are*, not just their choice of mate. Symbolic actions in the service will look and feel different because the principals are of the same gender. The couple may wish to add a "political" component/flavor to the service, using this time to advocate for civil marriage equality for all. While something ancient is being done (albeit in a new context), there are still some largely uncharted waters for clergy to navigate along the way.

Enjoy this book. Read it, dog-ear the pages, mark it up, send it to your parents and siblings. It's a book meant to be used. Its contents will spark discussion for the couple, helping them to understand the symbolic nature and power of what they are doing. No matter what form the final rite takes, the couple will know better *why* they are doing what they are doing. In the end, this book will make for a more genuine, authentic and heartfelt celebration for the couple and for those "tribes" who gather around the symbolic fire at the mouth of their cave to witness the joining of their children and friends in lifelong commitment.

—*V. Gene Robinson*

Ninth Episcopal Bishop of the
Diocese of New Hampshire

ACKNOWLEDGMENTS

WE HAVE RECEIVED MANY FORMS OF ASSISTANCE ON THIS PROJECT. Friends and colleagues encouraged us to fill the growing need for liturgical and pastoral care resources for ministry with same-gender loving couples. We are grateful to The Pilgrim Press and Kim Martin Sadler, our editor, whose support is consistent, flexible, and full of good humor. Kristin Firth's copyediting is done with an eye for accuracy and beauty and we applaud her gifts. Rick Porter's artistic sense made of our piled papers a graceful book. We are appreciative of the UCC Coalition for LGBT Concerns, as well as conference ministers throughout the United Church of Christ who publicized our call for submissions, and Darton, Longman, and Todd, Ltd., who connected us with British resources. The Northwood (New Hampshire) Congregational Church, UCC, has been generous with its gift of meeting space. We thank our friend the Rt. Rev. V. Gene Robinson, Bishop of New Hampshire, for his enthusiastic support as well as for writing the foreword. We especially thank Rev. Molly Baskette, Rev. Donald Schmidt, and Rev. Kathryn Schreiber, who were interviewed extensively for chapter 6; Rev. Dr. Fran Bogle, who searched out gifted writers; and all of those who have contributed their liturgical resources.

Countless social, religious, and political activists for marriage equality have shared with us their struggles and successes. We applaud their seemingly tireless dedication. And of course, there are so many couples who over the years have faced the difficulties we have tried to address and experienced the joys we hope to share with couples in the future.

Final thanks goes to readers, who are the ones who make this book come alive, and to clergy and couples alike who will make use of the different portions of this book. We wish you many blessings. Please use these resources freely in discussions, services, and ceremonies. Additional permission from The Pilgrim Press is only required for those who wish to reprint any portion of the text in a magazine, online, book, or paid public workshop.

Part One

Overview of the Issues

HE THINKS GAYS PUSHING TO GET MARRIED ARE DESTROYING THE SANCTITY OF OUR MARRIAGE, BUT I THINK IT'S HIS DRINKING, GAMBLING AND INFIDELITY.

Introduction

On July 19, 1991, my partner and I stood on the beach in Provincetown to speak our covenant of love and to promise our commitment to live together in spiritual marriage for the rest of our lives. The sun was setting on the horizon, the waves were breaking against the shore, and the birds were circling in the sky. We felt encompassed in sanctuary made holy by the gifts of creation and sanctified through the celebration and intention of love. A friend read scripture and played music. We spoke the vows of our hearts and minds and received a prayer of blessing. Upon leaving the beach we threw two yellow roses into the ocean and then took ourselves and our friends out for dinner. As I awoke the next morning, I experienced one of the oddest sensations of my life. I felt different. I looked at the woman in bed with me and sensed a new level of responsibility, concern, purpose, and awe. I felt both joy and terror as I wondered what I had gotten myself into. At the same time I was profoundly grateful.

Emily and I returned to establish our new home, which included two small children. We told our extended families the news. A glass was raised in one. No response in the other. We met with a lawyer to establish wills, trusts, powers of attorney, and guardianship of the children. We also returned to the rural congregations we had each been serving for several years, knowing that many of our parishioners would not affirm our relationship, and that some would. We each shared the news with a few parish members. No public affirmations were spoken, although privately we received some hugs and cheers. The ONA (Open and Affirming) movement was still new in the United Church of Christ, and neither of our churches had begun the process of study. We knew that we were at risk of losing our positions as parish pastors if we came out more and more about our relationship and family status. Sometimes I imagined how it might have been different in our churches and families had we been two heterosexual clergy getting married. The potlucks and showers would have lasted for months! The gifts to help us set up our household would have kept coming. The lawyer fees would have been minor, and the benefits attached to legal marriage are numerous. Nonetheless, we knew that we were spiritually married, that our covenant was sacred, and that, in our day-to-day loving of one another and our children, we would find God in our midst.

On January 1, 2008, at 12:01 A.M., a few hundred people gathered at the steps of the state capitol building in Concord, New Hampshire, to celebrate the passage of same-sex civil unions into state law. It was dark and cold at zero degrees, yet the energy and excitement was palpable. Speeches were offered and songs were sung. Spontaneous cheers and applause broke the chill. Clergy, justices of the peace, lawyers, and legislators affirmed the importance of working together to bring about social and legal change. The significance of legal civil unions was affirmed, along with the reminder that we were still in the struggle for full state and federal legal benefits and social recognition known only in the institution of marriage. Following the public ceremony, couples spread out across the statehouse lawn, in between snow banks and sidewalks, to ritualize their legal unions. Pastors and justices of the peace officiated as partners spoke their words of intention to each other. Some couples had been together for decades and others for months. Some brought friends and family, while others stood alone. Some prayed, some read poems, some cheered, some cried. Simultaneously, similar gatherings were held in many town squares and private homes across the state. CNN sent live video coverage across the country.

I served as the officiant for three couples that night. Throughout my career as a pastor, I have been theologically uncomfortable with the intermingling of church and state in the signing of marriage licenses. Why is it that clergy are expected to act as representatives of the government in the legal signing of marriage licenses, while in every other aspect of ministry, the boundary between religious and civil authority is clear? Why is it that a pastor's signature can render legal the rights and responsibilities of marriage, while the unbinding of the same legal status resides in the courts? To begin legal marriage, one may go to a pastor. To end it, one must go to court. When I officiate at same-sex legal civil unions and marriages I feel this same theological discomfort I experience at heterosexual weddings. After all, I have never been trained for nor called to a position in government. Nonetheless, officiating with a same-gender loving couple is an empowering place to serve in the quest for justice and equality. Although the theological concerns of power and authority remain the same, the playing field is closer to level between straight and gay. Thus, as I have signed same-sex marriage and civil union licenses, I sense the sacred call of a pastor in covenant with parishioners.

After seventeen years of spiritual marriage and family life, Emily and I were joined in a civil union that night at the statehouse. We had asked our pastor to officiate (calling him away from his family at New Year's), and met with him to plan the ceremony. During worship one Sunday, we shared our plans with the congregation, thanked the church for its advocacy and support in the legislative process to legalize same-sex relationships, and invited anyone who wanted to stand in the cold at midnight to join us. Emily and I decided that we wanted to speak the vows of marriage from the United Church of Christ Book of Worship to one another as a reaffirmation of our spiritual covenant. I knew a few close friends and family would stand with us, but I was not prepared for what actually happened. Despite the deep cold and the lateness of the hour, numerous members of our congregation came to stand with us. Some I might have guessed would show. However, many were a total surprise. I had no idea that Emily and I, the LGBTQ community, and our struggle for justice meant so much to so many. Everywhere I turned, someone I least expected was there with arms open for a hug and tears spilling in the joy of faithful community, family, and the gradual dismantling of oppression. I cried as I spoke my vows, holding onto Emily and tightly encircled by love.

The next morning when I awoke, something was different. However, it wasn't the same difference as that morning seventeen years ago in 1991, when we had spoken the first vows of our relationship. This new difference was not between Emily and me. Our spiritual marriage and deep love were not affected by this legal status or public ceremony. What had transpired was more social that personal in nature. Our union of hearts, bodies, minds, souls, goals, dreams, family, property, and finances now held some kind of legal status and general public affirmation. With the granting of civil unions, the power dynamic had begun to shift. Like when we ran into others' public disapproval, it seemed to feel less like our problem and more like theirs. Built into the law, our social status had changed. Granted, separate is not equal. Granted, the language of "civil union" rather than "marriage" creates unequal social and political power and respect. Yes, it is still second-class stature. Yet something is more than nothing. Having been accustomed to nothing, I have been surprised by the experience of internal healing that some level of public recognition provides.

In conversation with many LGBTQ persons, I have heard similar reactions expressed. Whether coupled or not, when oppressed individuals witness and participate in something that had categorically been denied them, healing happens. Perhaps years of internalized messages of shame are disempowered. The voices shouting that gay men cannot nurture families or that the love of lesbian couples is not real are silenced, even if for a time. The evidence stands clear that healthy, happy, same-gender loving couples have been and will continue to be living in our midst. Public ceremony ritualizes and confirms this. Liturgy within community solidifies support for the couple, affirming their bond within the larger human family. Therefore, whether it is a nonlegal ceremony of commitment within a community of friends, family, and congregation and/or a legally binding contract that sets apart two individuals as a family unit, the ceremony of covenant is critically important to the healing of internalized homophobia and institutionalized heterosexism.

At the 2009 Academy Awards, Dustin Black, the writer of the screenplay *Milk* chronicling the work of Harvey Milk and others for gay rights in San Francisco in the 1970s, won the award for best original screenplay. In his acceptance speech he said the following,:

> When I was thirteen years old, my beautiful mother and my father moved me from a conservative Mormon home in San Antonio, Texas, to California and I heard the story of Harvey Milk. And it gave me hope. It gave me the hope to live my life openly as who I am, and that maybe I could fall in love and one day get married.[1]

Although the specifics may vary, the dream of "falling in love and getting married" seems to be universal, transcending time, place, and culture. What Dustin Black's words speak to is the importance to the larger community of the experience of the couple. Certainly, lesbian, gay, bisexual, and transgender persons can meet and fall in love anywhere and anytime. Yet, as Dustin Black's words reveal, the dream, the vision, the longing is for public witness and affirmation. Yes, this is about the end of legal discrimination, but it is about more. It is about the end of social, cultural, and religious oppression. The experience of being exiled from a cultural dream cuts deep into one's psychological self-esteem and one's spiritual experience of and faith in a loving God. Conversely, public communal witness and validation of same-gender loving couples holds immense power to heal.

If "a rose is a rose by any other name," so is the love of one individual for another. Likewise is the human need for naming, witnessing, ritualizing, and affirming the love that for so many "dare not speak its name." Oppression runs deep. Yet, love continues to liberate.

—Leanne McCall Tigert

I

A Brief History of Marriage and Coupling in U.S. Church and Society

Ask anyone the question, "What is marriage?" and you will get an answer. The answer may be a familiar sounding rhetorical phrase, a personal antidote, or an academic discussion of emerging social constructs. Ask ten people, and you will get ten unique responses. Ask persons from different faith communities within the same major religion, and you might wonder whether or not you actually asked each of them the same question. If you read popular and academic books on the subject, you will surely get confused. Even in study, one's location in time and place creates a perspective that deeply affects and often determines the outcome. It seems that there are many competing and varied understandings, expressions, experiences, and definitions of marriage in our day and time. This is neither new nor unusual. The entity of marriage has been in fluid motion since its inception.

The concept of marriage has always held multiple meanings on many levels. Every two individuals joining in such a union bring their own understandings and must negotiate just what it is they are stepping into together. Once they are so joined, the meaning of a marriage will change over time, perhaps transforming into something unanticipated by the couple. Whenever two individuals come together in civil union, nonlegal covenant, or state sanctioned marriage, they join two family cultures. Customs, patterns, and traditions may collide with each other, and then be reinvented or forgotten. Of course, this was also true of the marriages and unions that went before them. Human history has been writing and rewriting the script of love and family bonding throughout time. Thus, the book of civil, religious, and emotional marriage is constantly in the process of editing a newly revised version.

Common arguments against legalizing same-sex marriage go something like "Gay marriage overturns thousands of years of history." "Same-sex marriage destroys the institution of marriage and family." "Marriage equals one man plus one woman." Each of these statements is both true and false, depending upon what, when, and to whom you look for evidence. For example, it is not difficult to find examples of legal marriages occurring between one man and several women, vows of love and companionship taken between two men, and the denial of marriage and family rights to heterosexual persons based upon social categories. Thus, one must be careful with any all-encompassing statements about historical precedent.

In addition, there are many possible responses to these statements and others like them, two of which are particularly important. First of all, the entity of marriage, its structure and purposes, have been in constant change. Yes, it is changing rapidly at this moment within our increasingly diverse society; however, in some sense this change is the cresting of a constant tide of motion. In his classic book *Same-sex Marriage: a Christian Ethical Analysis*, Marvin Ellison argues that any faithful discussion of marriage today must begin with an accurate understanding of history. Ellison states that when marriage "traditionalists" claim that same-sex marriage overturns thousands of years of an unchanging tradition and history, they refuse to employ basic historical research and analysis, and they ignore what historians, social scientists, and anthropologists continue to discover. Without accurate historical and cultural awareness we have no way to authentically locate our understandings of the present. In this way, we can easily deny effective and liberating change in our time.

> A historical sensibility is especially needed to offset claims by self-described traditionalists who refrain from using a historical method.

> . . . Despite such ahistorical claims, marriage as an institution has assumed a variety of forms and served purposes quite different from those familiar to contemporary North Americans . . . marriage must be carefully placed in historical and cultural context. Otherwise, we might miss taking into account an insight that informs all social change movements: the way things are is not the way things must be. Whatever is can be undone or at least modified through collective human agency.[1]

More importantly, change is not destruction. Change is a constantly occurring process that claims and reclaims something for the long run and, hopefully, for the common good. As the old adage states, one must "change or die." Life is not static. As humans change, so do human institutions, no matter how sacred. Perhaps the growing movement of same-gender loving couples seeking public legal and religious recognition is not the death rattle of the institution of marriage. Indeed, it might signal the end of marriage as we have known it to be an exclusivist, sexist, and heterosexist institution.

Perhaps the present movement for same-sex marriage is more like a midwife—seeking to deliver something new and energetic, saving marriage from the cultural death of cynicism, irrelevance, and oppression. As in any birth, it is calling each of us in this shared human family to join together in nurturing new life, and then to step back with wonder, joy, and a little anxiety to watch just how this new life will step out on its own, and where it will lead us in the generations to come. In other words, same-gender loving couples joining in publicly recognized civil and religious unions do not threaten to destroy the institution of marriage. However, they do change it, and so become a chapter in the ever evolving story of human and divine love.

There have been many definitions, expressions, and functions of the institution of marriage throughout time. Although the study of marriage over thousands of years and across multiple cultures greatly enhances and expands the reality of this commonly held belief, even within modern Western society, one finds this dynamic to be true. Legal scholar Evan Wolfson defines marriage as "Primarily a committed relationship of two people, recognized and supported by the state, who undertake a commitment and who receive important protections and benefits, and also obligations and responsibilities"[2] Anthropologist Edmund Leach writes that marriage governs property and status through "the set of legal rules . . . handed down from generation to generation"[3]

Although these definitions may leave us less than inspired, most of us hear a ring of truth in them. Even within the different understandings of marriage today, most of us agree that it currently involves two individuals freely choosing to join their lives together as the result of romantically falling in love and intending to care for one another throughout the remainder of their lives. Who gets to do this, what rights and responsibilities come with it, and how it is undone have become the focus of our present day disagreements, fueling the energy of our debates. Interestingly, these shared notions of romance, marriage, and coupling we hold dear in our culture seem fairly new in the course of human history. In her book *Marriage, A History,* Stephanie Coontz, author and director of Research and Public Education at the Council on Contemporary Families, writes the following:

> As I researched further and consulted with colleagues studying family life around the world, I came to believe that the current rearrangement of both married and single life is in fact without historical precedent . . . when it comes to the overall place of marriage in society and the relationship between husbands and wives, nothing in the past is anything like what we have today.[4]

Thus, the experience of marriage has been changing rapidly and continues to do so. This was true before the present movement of same-gender loving couples seeking public, legal, and religious recognition, and will continue with or without gay marriage.

In the long view of history, our present concept of marriage as a choice born out of the romantic love of two people is very new. Until recently, love was seen as a possible, but not necessary, outcome rather than prerequisite, of marriage. In some cultures, it was believed that shared passion and eroticism between legal spouses was inappropriate or even impossible, and it became suspect. Coontz and others point to Greek and Roman philosophers who asserted that any husband who loved his wife too much became an adulterer. Plato often spoke of the power of true love to inspire. However, he was writing about the experience one man could share with another. Perhaps it never occurred to him that women might feel as deeply as men. Stories from European society during the middle and early modern ages are rife with tales of passion outside the bonds of marriage, and misery within. The demands of joining kingdoms and property, and the goals of stabilizing political, economic, and social power through brokered marriages far outweighed consideration of any one individual's happiness.

The list could go on and on, citing example after example of the insignificance of personal choice and emotion in the institution of marriage. No matter how long the list becomes, two truths emerge. First, for most of Western history the experience of romantic love between individuals and the social and legal functions of marriage had little to do with one another. Second, the history of sexism keeping women out of positions of power in church and society colluded in this separation of romantic love from marriage. Women were held at bay from court and pulpit and were often viewed as extraneous to higher forms of love. Procreative sex and the raising of children were for marriage. Passion and eroticism were to be found in affairs, while the more abiding emotion of love was often saved for friendships between men. The breaking of these rules and mores has given us fairy tales, epic historical novels, and powerful role models in women and men through the ages. Perhaps those who broke the rules separating romance from marriage—most of whom were heterosexual—are the ones responsible for the present-day struggles in defining marriage. We are simply building on what has gone before.

Although this chapter cannot describe in detail all of the research concerning marriage during human history, suffice it to say that there is much available, as is evidenced in the works cited. As we look across the long arc of the history of marriage, research overwhelmingly describes the traditions of marriage as those of prioritizing property contracts, settling political disputes, structuring extended family kinships, and providing a division of labor. These functions created social stability, yet few in our time, gay or straight, would affirm that this is what we want. The term "traditional marriage" has become a euphemism for heterosexual marriage, modeled upon the radically new idea of marrying for love, which is neither traditional nor historical at all. In fact, two heterosexual adults freely choosing to live together and/or marry one another for love has much more in common with the same-sex partnerships of today than with a long history of traditional marriages brokered without love.

Marriage has evolved over time, and same-sex marriage can be understood as a logical step in this constantly changing process. Today, marriage is a fragile institution, not because same-gender loving couples are seeking to be married, but because technological, social, cultural, and environmental changes have made marriage harder to sustain in either past or present forms. During these last two hundred years, technology has advanced so rapidly that it continuously shifts how we work, play, and build relationships with one another. Of course, this is true with many of our social institutions today. Leaders in economics, law, education, and religion are scrambling to understand our changing local, global, and environmental realities in order to create new methodologies and technologies relevant to today's lived experience. "Sustainability" has become a rallying call for many behaviors, patterns, and technologies we once took for granted. Reflecting on her research concerning marriage, Coontz continues,

> Everywhere marriage is becoming more optional and more fragile. Everywhere, the once-predictable link between marriage and child rearing is fraying. And everywhere, relationships between men and women are undergoing rapid and at times traumatic transformation . . . the relations between men and women have changed more in the last thirty years than in the last three thousand.[5]

In the eighteenth century, the significance of love as the primary reason for marriage in our culture began to take shape. Prior to this, marriage was viewed as far too critical to the economic and political welfare of a society to be left in the hands of individuals moved by emotion and sentimentality. As personal choice came to the forefront in establishing marriage, so did the fragility of marriage grow. For little more than two hundred years, love has been acknowledged as the most fundamental reason from marriage, with one's satisfaction and fulfillment becoming the barometer by which to measure marital success. Thus, the same value placed on love as the primary reason for marriage creates an inherent instability not known prior to this experience. Again, according to Stephanie Coontz,

> As soon as the idea that love should be the central reason for marriage, and companionship its basic goal, was first raised, observers of the day warned that the same values that increased people's satisfaction with marriage as a relationship had an inherent tendency to undermine the stability of marriage as an institution. The very features that promised to make marriage such a unique and treasured personal relationship opened the way for it to become an optional and fragile one.[6]

In no way does this suggest that instability in and of itself is bad and that, therefore, we should return to the arranged marriages of yesterday. It simply states that along with many other structures and constructs of our social order, marriage and coupling are shifting at rapid speed in both purpose and form. The emergence of the field of psychology has changed both modern insight into and value placed upon emotional well-being. This development is so new that it creates difficulties in understanding and communication between generations even today.

Psychologist Mary Pipher points out in her book *Another Country: Navigating the Emotional Terrain of our Elders* that language, beliefs, and knowledge differ so much between the "baby boomers" and their parents from "the greatest generation" as to render communication about family concerns and care across these generational lines fraught with difficulties.[7] As a baby boomer with young adult children, I experience this dynamic in conversing with the next generation as well. Our children's children may speak an entirely different language about love and family, needing yet a different set of relational skills and social structures.

Current research on brain function, emotional regulation, and happiness are changing many of our perceptions about personal relationship skills needed for long-term coupling. If we are to support the marriages and covenants of love today and tomorrow, we must understand the fragility of love between two persons and find creative ways to affirm their radical and often scary choice to partner together.

Hundreds of years ago, when the human life span was more than thirty years shorter than today, legal marriages lasted a lifetime but excluded many from partnering with the person of their choosing. Therefore, they really cannot help us with our present dilemmas. Marriage and union today affirm our cultural values in the same way that marriage in the past affirmed the dominant social values of that day. Some of these values—reverence of the divine, the importance of both community identity and personal integrity—remain the same. Yet, the ways we describe God or define community and integrity continue to shift. To be human is to know erotic energy, whether in the compelling artistry of the colors of sunset, the joy of perfectly blended musical instruments, or the body's immediate response to a passionate kiss. Perhaps if we hold fast to these core experiences and values of humanity across the ages, we can liberate civil contracts and religious covenants from the limited view of our own immediate perspective.

While it is true that marriage and coupling have multiple meanings and expressions across the world and throughout time, even within the brief span of U.S. history, marriage laws have served political and social functions and have changed with our understandings and values. In the country's early years, marriage was a right belonging only to property holders, who, by definition, were white men.[8] The realities of sexism and racism were written into marriage laws at the beginning of the nation and have required significant social movements for change. Often these changes took place one step at a time, not unlike the struggle for LGBTQ liberation.

Many historians assert that our country's founders considered marriage to be a civil ceremony conveying certain civil rights, which in turn established working units of obligation and connection. Andrew Chertin, PhD, professor of sociology at John Hopkins University, describes one purpose of marriage in colonial times to be the creation of the "public family" functioning as "school, house of correction, orphanage, nursing home, or poorhouse."[9] In the same vein, Stephanie Coontz goes so far as to say, "Probably the single most important function of marriage through most of history, although it is completely eclipsed today, was its role in establishing cooperative relationships between families and communities."[10] In the establishment of a new country, legal marriage would have played such a role in the forming of communities and the creation of new social, legal, and economic networks. Coontz continues:

> Marriage usually determines rights and obligations connected to sexuality, gender roles, relationships with in-laws, and the legitimacy of children. It also gives the participants specific rights and roles within the larger society. It usually defines the mutual duties of husband and wife and often the larger duties of their respective families toward each other, and it makes those duties enforceable. It also allows the property and status of the couple or household head to be passed down to the next generation in an orderly manner.[11]

In the United States marriage has always been a political act, regulating who can marry whom, and who then becomes related to and responsible for whom. For most of our history, this regulation has been based on race and/or gender.

One manifestation of the painful reality of racism within our country has been the history of marriage inequality for people of color. Throughout the horror of slavery, African, Caribbean, African-American, and Caribbean-American slaves were prohibited from legal marriage and the establishment of legally recognized family bonds. As with any oppressed community, this does not mean that spiritual and emotional marriage did not take place, nor did it prevent the community from recognizing and celebrating these bonds of companionship. Wilma A. Dunaway, author of *The African-American Family in Slavery and Emancipation*, describes extensive family rituals and patterns among slave communities, despite all that conspired against them.[12] Numerous historians have discovered a vast array of cultural patterns and rituals in coupling, depending upon the practices of one's particular racial and ethnic home.

If, as Coontz asserts, marriage has functioned to establish rights and obligations, then the prevention of marriage and family bonds between persons of color held in bondage functioned to maintain the power and privilege of white slave owners and deepen the institutionalization of racism in family law. Research shows that African and Caribbean families brought with them extensive family networks, which were intentionally disrupted by slavery, yet continued to survive. It is commonly known that slave owners and traders would routinely separate adult partners from one another, parents from children, and siblings from each other. Even so, the covenants of love could not be extinguished. Essentially, the practice of enslaving people of color colluded with the prevention of all women from voting and land ownership to create plantations and households based on the premise that all persons are to be loyal and submissive to only the white male head of household.[13]

In 1664, Maryland legally prohibited marriage between white women and black men. In 1705, a Massachusetts law was enacted to ban interracial marriage. Other states followed, resulting in a total of at least forty preventing marriage between persons of different races, a legal ban that continued unabated until 1948, when the court system of California became the first in the nation to rule the interracial ban in marriage illegal and unconstitutional. Ellison states that due to the "unfettered power of Jim Crow segregation at the time, the decision was widely denounced as threatening the stability of Western civilization." It took twenty more years for the Supreme Court to issue a decision declaring marriage to be a "personal vital right," thus declaring state laws preventing interracial marriage between men and women to be illegal.[14]

Many of today's arguments opposing the legalization of same-sex marriage and full recognition of same-gender loving couples proclaim that marriage and family require "one man and one woman." This belief comes, in part, from generations of sexist ideology that has defined and limited both women and men. Often, this unchallenged sexism is rooted in assumptions about the nature of psychological gender and biological sex. In other words, we assume that genetically born men and women are different not only in primary and secondary sex characteristics, but also in their experience of being human. This binary gender construct provides the foundation of our beliefs about women and men as opposites. In turn, this opposition assumes that in order for a marriage to be whole, it must include both a man and a woman. As Virginia Ramey Mollenkott writes in her book *Omnigender: A Trans-religious Approach*:

> Throughout the centuries of heteropatriarchy, the concept of two opposite sexes has served as a boundary to hold in place the established patterns of power. The binary gender construct has dictated that real males must be naturally drawn to those attitudes, behaviors, and roles any given society considers "masculine," including sexual attraction to females only. And real females must be naturally drawn to those behaviors, attitudes, and roles any given society considers "feminine," including sexual attraction to males only. . . . The binary gender construct is assumed to be The Way Things Ought to Be—the order of creation, the will of God, unchangeable and beyond question.[15]

In Western European and North American societies, these divisions have been delineated clearly as those inside the home and outside the home. Men's "appropriate" sphere of action has been that of politics and macroeconomics, while women have been relegated to management within the household. In postcolonial times, as marriage became privatized and women's lives became more narrowly focused on homemaking, this belief in gender complementarity became more ensconced. Marvin Ellison refers to the work of John D'Emilio and Estelle B. Freedman in describing the role of "the good wife" as one who nurtured children and provided care for her husband in order to create for him "a safe haven from the fiercely competitive male world of capitalist economic expansion."[16]

Over time, the assumptions of this binary gender construct have been upheld by laws of property, finance, employment, housing, and marriage, as well as incorporated into social expectations, customs, and mores. Actually, in organizing opposition to same-sex marriage, the present coalescing of religious evangelicals and fundamentalists with conservative political activists has reversed many of the positive steps the women's movement has taken out of this gender construct, seemingly to return us to a nostalgic view of times when "men were men and girls were girls."

This insistence on the necessity of men and women to complement each other in relationship has found rationalization and support in various circles of theology. In some arguments, women have been viewed as the evil temptresses of devout and holy men. In other arguments, women are considered holy and pure, more capable than men of nurturing children and keeping the family sacred and safe from the evils of the world. While sounding counter to one another, both of these perceptions serve the function of gender complementarity. First, men and women need each other, but neither gets to choose just how this connection might work in terms of individual roles, skills, and preferences. Second, in neither of these belief systems do women get to leave the house. There is neither mutuality nor shared power. Rosemary Radford Ruether describes what has become known as the "Cult of Domesticity":

> A new religious ideology imagined the home as a magic circle of pure womanhood, and innocent childhood, as unfallen Garden of Eden set against a sinful male realm of business and politics . . . [women became] nurturers of a prolonged childhood and healers of the bruised egos of men. . . . In effect, middle-class America gave up trying to create a godly society and retreated to making a godly home.[17]

While this argument for the necessity of two opposite genders has been used primarily to oppress women, sometimes it has been used as a rationale for equality based in the notion that the balancing of qualities and characteristics of men and women is necessary for personal and political well-being. In this vein, activists opposed to same-sex marriage will decry that difference does not imply good and bad, or that one is valued more than the other. They state that this simply means that men and women need each other. On the surface this might be appealing. However, the reality is that one's gender identity may fall anywhere along a continuum of male/female rather than within a strict category defined by physically observable sex characteristics. Neither is everyone heterosexual. According to more recent scientific and medical research and feminist, queer, liberation, and postmodern theologies and psychologies, these supposed differences are not universally true. At the same time, separate is not equal in the world of money and power. In a capitalist society, whoever holds the money holds the social and legal power connected to it. Thus, by virtue of their social capital in this scenario, men get to define the rules, thereby deciding what is "male" and "female." Again, "a rose by any other name is still a rose." No matter what one calls it, constricting choice based on perceived qualities and characteristics of gender and sex is oppressive and discriminatory.

In 1987, another page in the history of legal marriage in the United States was turned, shedding light on the present struggles of same-gender loving couples. The Supreme Court overturned a state law denying prisoners the right to marry. This decision was founded upon the court's understanding of marriage as a human and civil right and, therefore, not deniable based upon a category or class of citizenship. Marvin Ellison writes that in its description as a human right, the court included the following characteristics of marriage:

- An expression of emotional support and public commitment;
- For some, an act with spiritual significance, and for some, the exercise of a religious faith;
- A relationship with the expectation that, for most, the marriage will be consummated; and
- A relationship that can receive tangible benefits, including government benefits and property rights.[18]

It is not difficult to see the implications this has for the legal marriage of same-gender loving couples. If marriage is truly a human right for all citizens, including prisoners, equally then it must be a human right for all gay, lesbian, bisexual, and transgender citizens.

One of the defining characteristics of being human is that of the emotion of love in all its many and varied forms. As long as there have been people, there has been love. As long as there has been love, there have been relationships of love. As long as there have been relationships of love, there have been same-gender loving couples. Even though the concept of sexual orientation is a modern understanding originating in the seventeenth century, there have been accounts of same-sex lifetime partnering and homosexual sexual behavior long before this. Understandings of gender identity and expression are even more recent than that of sexual orientation, and yet, relationships between persons of various gender identities and expressions have also existed throughout human history. Perhaps the biggest problem with gaining full knowledge of the history of nonheterosexual love and relationships concerns the lack of recorded information about this in the annals of history.

In their book *Heterosexism in Contemporary World Religion*, editors Marvin Ellison and Judith Plaskow write, "All religions suffer from amnesia. They can forget their better moments in the past when prejudice did not dull their vision. . . . Religions also suffer from contagion."[19] The book continues with the work of several scholars writing about the evidence of LGBTQ persons as well as their oppression and repression within the large span of world religions. Examples within Islam and Hinduism, Confucianism and Taoism, along with Judaism and Christianity, are cited. It seems that at various times in the near and distant past, most religions have had moments both of supporting and oppressing queer love. Unfortunately, the power of heterosexism seems to be more contagious than the affirmation of love in all its diversity.

Although research into the history of queer love is relatively new, many secular and religious scholars have pointed to similar findings. There is evidence of erotic love and lifetime companioning between partners of the same sex/gender across cultures, throughout time, and in all religions, even as far back as 12,000 B.C.E. As is true in the experience of oppressed communities, the truth about the real lives of LGBTQ persons over time is little known, not because it did not happen, but because it has been kept out of the mainstream of recorded history. Due to actual and feared recrimination, much of the writing of these erotic and passionate connections between same-sex lovers is poetic, symbolic, and ambiguous. Other writings that may have been romantic and sexual have been misinterpreted as spiritual and symbolic. Unfortunately, much has been lost as generations have passed without lifting the veil of heterosexism that rendered their love unspeakable.

In the United States, the modern gay rights movement claims its roots in the Stonewall riot of 1969. On June 28 of that year, police raided the Stonewall Inn in the Greenwich Village neighborhood of New York City. Although raids and harassment were not unusual, fighting back was. On that particular night something new happened. While being clubbed and forced into police paddy wagons, the bar patrons fought back, perhaps in sheer frustration and the exhaustion that oppression yields. In this act of rebellion, a new community empowerment and activism was born, claiming civil and human rights. Ever since, LGBTQ persons and allies have organized June Pride Days in cities across the country in celebration of queer lives and in empowerment for the ongoing struggle for full equality.

During the 1960s, secular and religious gay rights support and advocacy groups were organizing in multiple cities, giving rise to the emerging political and social networks of the seventies and the activism of the eighties and beyond. Although there was little focus in these earlier years on same-sex marriage rights, the importance of the connections made for couples during this time cannot be overstated. As individuals came out, they began to discover a larger number of couples and families among them than even they might have imagined. As couples and families came together, they began to speak about their experiences to one another. The silence was broken as people shared the joys and challenges of love in the midst of a heterosexist and homophobic society. Partners talked with partners. Parents spoke with parents. Children found others like themselves. Isolation and fear gave way to community and hope. In turn, the LGBTQ movement for civil, religious, and human rights began to address the legal and social needs of these couples and families.

In various states, cities, and towns, gay and lesbian couples began to organize for laws protecting the relationships between same-sex partners and LGBTQ parents and children. The wave of change began with countless ripples of action and is continuing to swell with every move toward the full and mutual recognition of all couples and families, without regard to sex and gender. In the forward to the book *Lesbians and Gays in Couples and Families*, highly respected family therapist Monica McGoldrick writes,

> They questioned, and they (gay men) moved themselves beyond the dominant society's rigid, stultifying, deadening roles for men. . . . Gay men have helped teach us what being a "real man"—husband, father, lover, brother, son—can be about. Likewise, lesbians are teaching the heterosexual world about developing true partnership

> in relationship, partnerships that can help move us toward a new world order of equity in relationships—relationships in which a hierarchy of power is not the primary definer. . . . Our closed-mindedness about gays and lesbians has been so detrimental . . . that it has led us into a falsely closed, oversimplified life pattern and inhibited our human potential. We have drawn false maps of human psychology and of family connections. By remaining ignorant about gays and lesbians and their families, we have remained ignorant both about ourselves and those with whom we work, whether they are straight or gay.[20]

In some sense, we are riding the perfect storm in the movement toward full equality of same-gender loving couples. As queer people come out, connect, acknowledge, bless, and legalize their unions, the state of marriage and coupling changes for all. As patterns of and beliefs about heterosexual coupling and marriage shift, the changing face of marriage and family affects everyone. As transgender persons challenge cultural assumptions about the varied layers of gender identity and expression, the roles of men and women in relation to themselves and each other deepen and grow.

The more we share with one another about the real nature of our relationships and covenants, the more we will realize how much we have in common, whatever our sexual orientation and gender identity might be. The more we share in common, the less we will hold to our fears of those who are different. Perhaps it is not the "state of marriage" about which we should be speaking. Rather, it is the "mosaic of marriage" that we see—a work of art created through the richness of hue and diversity of color. The elements of creation come together, enriching one another as light shifts, changing as material settles over time. What we see at any one time may not be what stands out at the next viewing, depending upon our own perspective. The question "What is marriage?" receives a variety of answers. However, we need not be afraid. As Paul reminds us in his letter to the congregation at Corinth, "Love never ends" (1 Cor. 13:8).

2

Loving Relationships: Looking for Love and Relationships in the Bible

If "What is marriage?" receives an array of confusing answers, "What does the Bible say about same-sex marriage and same-gender loving couples?" does as well. There are not only a multitude of different and opposing answers, there are also different types of answers. Some will be only a few words long, such as, "It condemns it," or "I don't care," or "It's irrelevant to me." All of these prevent real conversation. Other replies may be paragraphs in explanation of one's own beliefs, supported by memorized quotations from the translation or interpretation of choice. Some may acknowledge that the Bible is confusing, depending upon what particular book or passage one reads at any given moment. Still others may suggest that people can use the Bible to support any position on any argument, if they dig deep enough. A few might ask you, "Old [First] Testament or New [Second] Testament?"

Inevitably, someone will respond with, "Jesus never mentioned sexual orientation." By the end of these interactions, you may find yourself exhausted with the burden of it all and stop asking the questions altogether. Yet, like many, you cannot stop these questions inside your own mind. Even if you are not a person of faith nor have ever had any connection with a religious community, present-day interpretations of the Hebrew and Christian scriptures affect you. Ideas, beliefs, stories, and images from the Bible reverberate throughout our culture. Ignoring this is risky. Oversimplifying is perilous.

Whatever your experience with the Bible and questions of same-gender loving couples, if you are a person of Christian faith, you should not simply walk away, refusing to engage. For better and for worse, these are our shared sacred texts. In fact, these are the texts that bind us to our Muslim and Jewish sisters and brothers in their faiths, for we are all people of "the Book." These texts have continued to stand as the primary record of our early faith history. Like all recordings of history, they may be the dominant story, but not the only story.

Whether you are a partner in a same-gender loving couple; pastor or spiritual care giver; family member, friend, or ally; or a curious bystander, it is critical to understand how your own experience of faith and scripture have formed you into the sexual and spiritual person that you are. It is also important to be aware of the appeals to scripture in secular and civil debates regarding the legislative process and ensuing decisions affecting the lives of all LGBTQ persons. An openly gay, avowed atheist lawyer who gives tirelessly of himself to the legislative work of seeking justice for LGBTQ persons once said, "We'll never get anywhere without the churches." In turn, the churches, families, and couples of Christian faith will not get far without a relationship of integrity with scripture.

If you ask a number of people how they read the Bible, you will likely get a variety of responses indicative of a multitude of approaches that may seem overwhelming. However, we are a collection of many and varied people. As long as we each understand and take responsibility for our own interpretations and lenses through which we view scripture, as long as we listen respectfully to others describe their interpretations and lenses, then we can communicate, possibly growing into more complete understanding together. The only response that cuts off the conversation is some version of "I read the Bible the right way, God's way" (which actually means "my way"). Obviously, this kind of response sets up a barrier, around which fruitful communication is impossible. Unfortunately, this is true whether we are trying to connect with family members about a same-gender loving couple's choice of covenant or are speaking with a disaffected church member.

At this point the content becomes less relevant, while the process must take center stage. This is always true when we try to engage in difficult conversations about conflictual topics. Nevertheless, as families and as congregations, we are often connected to those who think, feel, and act differently than ourselves; and yet we value our connection with them. Naming both the goal and process of communication is critical if these situations are to become open gates of sharing rather than locked fences of difference.

Although none of us can take responsibility for someone else's behavior, we can and must claim our own. Again, we start this process with our own experience and learn the tools to engage scripture seriously. From here, our relationship with the Bible is one of integrity, neither rigid nor stagnant. As we focus on our own deepening process, we are freed from the burden of convincing others. Then, in the language of the Difficult Conversations model of conflict negotiation,[1] we are empowered to advocate for the story of our relationship with scripture. In other words, we explain, clarify, and present it as clearly as we can, and let go of trying to make it everyone else's. This becomes the starting point of shared dialogue that heals instead of harms.

APPROACHES TO AND RELATIONSHIPS WITH THE BIBLE

If we each have a unique relationship with the Bible, what are some of these common approaches to scripture from which we draw? What are possible relationships that individuals, couples, and congregations may have with the written words of the Bible? As usual, there are several answers to this question.

Too often, we approach scripture the same way we read a textbook, scanning the words for "the right answer." This approach assumes that, if we read a portion and memorize it, then we can do exactly what it tells us to, and we will have solved our problem. However, the Bible is neither a playbook nor an instructional manual. Yes, there are some passages with detailed technical instruction, such as how to build an ark in case of flood or prepare a goat for sacrifice. Additionally, one can find authoritative directives ordering women to be silent in worship or slaves to obey their masters. Hopefully, these are irrelevant to our day and time. Even so, whether liberal or conservative, whether by unconscious habit or conscious effort, we sometimes throw cursory glances at the words of scripture without engaging the larger themes. In other words, we miss the forest for the trees. Perhaps we do this to refute others or to calm our own anxiety. Sometimes we do this because taking scripture seriously requires much intellectual, emotional, and spiritual work. Like any relationship of merit, our connection with the Bible requires self-awareness and attentive energy to make it worthwhile.

The literalist approach to the Bible, which lifts words and stories out of their cultural, historical, and literary context, forms the foundation for many of the arguments against the full recognition of same-gender loving couples. Usually, people do not claim that they are using this approach, as it has become associated with fundamentalism, and actually is impossible to use. First of all, we are not conversant in the original spoken or written language of biblical times. Secondly, a true literal approach is consistent only if we follow every word, literally. Yet, due to the inconsistencies from one passage to another, this is not possible. Finally, most would not want to follow every word, especially those that instruct the leverage of severe physical and mental pain as punishment for perceived transgressions. As John Boswell and other biblical scholars have pointed out, people pick and choose in scripture.

> The very same books which are thought to condemn homosexual acts condemn hypocrisy in the most strident terms . . . and yet, society did not create any social taboos against hypocrisy, did not claim that hypocrites were "unnatural," did not segregate them into an oppressed minority, did not enact laws punishing their sin with castration or death. No Christian state, in fact, has passed laws against hypocrisy per se, despite its continual and explicit condemnation by Jesus and the church. In the very same list which has been claimed to exclude from the kingdom of heaven those guilty of homosexual practices, the greedy are also excluded. And yet no medieval states burned the greedy at the stake.[2]

Something else is at play here—something that has allowed multiple cultures and communions to create and believe conclusions unsupported, and even untenable, to the essence of the very scripture being quoted. Two significant but often unspoken dynamics affecting our approach to the study of scripture and same-gender loving couples come from the combination of our tendency to avoid confusion and complexity coupled with internalized scripts of negativity and shame toward sexuality.

Dr. Peter Gomes, American Baptist minister faculty member at the Harvard Divinity School, writes, "Contemporary Christians tend to avoid complexity as being hazardous to their faith, and are thus unprepared to cope with complexity when it confronts them."[3] There is truth to this. Our daily lives can be so overwhelming and confusing that we want our spiritual lives to be simple. If we feel stressed out at work, we want to relax on our Sabbath. If we feel "bad" at work, we want to feel "good" at church. As a parish pastor said to me, "People are so battered by the world that the only thing they want to hear me preach is, 'God loves you, God loves you, God loves you,' and nothing else." Thus, when it comes to scripture we may opt for superficiality over struggle. Those of us who count ourselves as liberal and progressive can see and name this superficiality at work when conservatives and fundamentalists shout slogans such as "Adam and Eve—not Adam and Steve." We hear it in statements like "The Bible and Jesus define marriage as between one man and one woman. The church cannot condone or bless same-sex marriages because this stands in opposition to Scriptures and our tradition."[4] In these instances, such complex avoidant behavior is dangerous, giving rise to oppression, discrimination, and harm.

Liberal and progressive people of faith can also oversimplify complex biblical realities. How often do couples—gay, straight, and transgender—read passages about love at a wedding or covenanting ceremony, listening to only the poetic sweetness floating to the top, skimming over the challenging ethic of love of God, neighbor, and self that provides its very foundation? We, too, find ourselves lifting passages out of context, avoiding the call to ground life with our partner in a life of service to God and neighbor. Pastors oversimplify in an effort to be supportive of couples who may have weathered much confrontation just to come to this moment in their lives.

The binding covenant of love is joyful, but not simple. It is intimate, but not isolating. In these instances, the avoidance of complexity is deadening and robs us of the chance to live into the fullness of our faith. Professor and author Ronald E. Long describes biblical tradition as one reflecting a combination of the prophetic revolution and the pursuit of justice, and yet, "In modern times, the church has in contrast more often than not defended the status quo over against change . . . the bulk of the faithful have as often as not defended the practices they have grown too comfortable with to challenge."[5] Thus, whatever our intention, when we avoid ambiguity, complexity, or depth, we bypass the opportunity to join our lives with biblical writers who have struggled before us, and we miss the chance to join that "so great a cloud of witnesses [who] lay aside every weight and the sin that clings so closely, and . . . run with perseverance the race that is set before us" (Heb. 12:1).

In addition to complacency and fears of complexity, we each bring our experiences and understandings of sexuality to any engagement with the Bible. To our detriment, the historical and modern church has been sorely deficient in educating and enabling its members to develop healthy sexual identities. The historical teachings of the church, invoking the authority of scripture, have not been passively neutral in this deficiency, but have been actively harmful, often leading the charge against those who challenge the sexual mores of any given day and age. For generations, we have internalized cultural and religious scripts of sexual shame and fear that teach us to condemn and control erotic energy or be destroyed by it.

These scripts have separated the passion of the earthly Jesus from the passion of our own earthly bodies. Church tradition has often taught that our bodies and our sexual selves are somehow intrinsically bad, embarrassing, ugly, and even evil—and in some instances, thus deserving of punishment. Despite our core Christian affirmation that God became incarnate in the "flesh" as Jesus, we denigrate the body as the antithesis of God, something to be overcome, whose natural urges must be denied if we are to become spiritually faithful. Sexual shame can be understood as the emotional experience of feeling exposed, vulnerable, humiliated, wrong, or bad within our deepest embodied selves, not because of what we do, but just because of who we are, in our erotic, messy, and passionate body-selves. Sadly, many of us internalize this sexual shame in the core of our being. In my previous book, *Coming Out through Fire*, the impact of this shame is described:

> Shame in the lives of gay/lesbian/bisexual/transgender persons . . . is the source of much of our pain—emotionally, spiritually, sexually, individually, and socially. It prevents healthy self-esteem, impedes our ability to form loving and intimate relationships, and blocks a healthy knowing of ourselves as beloved children of God, created in God's image. . . . In all of this we are no different from heterosexuals—sexual shame fuels fear and the need to control.[6]

These messages of shame and fear of the body can and must be named in order to be replaced with messages of joyful acceptance and celebration of all that makes us earthly children of God. We must internalize new scripts that rejoice in the gift of embodiment and affirm the diversity of sexual and gender identify as an expression of the diverse creativity of our loving God. As Jim Nelson writes,

> If the imago Dei is love manifested within us, and if our true identities are to be found in and through embodied relationships, we must learn to love the flesh. God in the flesh; in our own flesh; in the enfleshed neighbor near and far, the human neighbor and the earth itself as our neighbor.[7]

Again, whether you are a partner of a same-gender loving couple, a pastor or spiritual care giver, a family member, friend, or ally, or a curious bystander, it is critical that you name whatever sexual scripts you have internalized from religion and society. Then you will be able to look at these texts with fresh eyes, seeing the authors of scripture as human beings with their own internalized messages of their day. In turn, this may free you up to note the passionate, erotic, life-affirming Word of God between, among, and within the written words of humans.

Given this combination of the complexities of our modern lives, the lack of meaningful sexually affirming teachings and experiences within communities of faith, and the cultural and religious scripts of sexual shame we have internalized over time, it is no wonder that we have trouble engaging the Bible seriously in questions of understanding and supporting same-gender loving couples. It is amazing that we can engage the Bible at all in matters of sexuality. Yet, we can, we do, and we must if we are to foster couples and communities of healthy sexuality and spirituality, joyously celebrating the embodied and erotic love of God in whom we live, move, and have our being.

A RELATIONAL SEXUALITY AND APPROACH TO SCRIPTURE

During the past few decades, biblical scholars and theologians have done remarkable work in the interpretation of scripture and homosexuality. Using the tools of historical, cultural, literary, and genealogical criticism, similar findings have emerged from many endeavors. For our focus on the covenanting of same-gender loving couples, a few of themes are very important.

First of all, the concepts of sexuality and sexual orientation that we use in modern and postmodern thought would have been completely alien to those of biblical times. "Sexuality" is a medical and psychological construct consisting of our identity and expression of gender, the experience and orientation of our erotic attraction, our physical/biological sex, and the social expectations and cultural norms pertaining to sex and gender.[8] We speak of sexuality as part of our psychological identity. In contrast, biblical writers thought and wrote without any of these medical, psychological, or sociological constructs.

Very little is said in scripture about homosexuality and same-gender loving couples. As far as we know, Jesus said nothing on the subject. In all of scripture there are a few descriptions of same-sex sex acts, and no references to sexual orientation, gender identity, or long-term committed same-gender loving partners. Due to their misuse by those who condemn queer people today, the seven passages of scripture that directly mention homosexual behavior are known by many as the "texts of terror." The mention of these few same-sex sexual behaviors occurs within stories of violence, exploitation, fear for survival in the face of enemies, and/or rape. Obviously, actions of sexual, physical, emotional, or cultural violence should never be condoned, whatever one's sexual orientation or gender identity.

Second, no matter how vigorously some people defend "one man plus one woman" as the biblical model of family, nothing could be further from the data. Biblical families are many and varied. Even the idea of coupling and family life is not always held in high esteem. Biblical scholars point to the recorded words of the never married Jesus spread throughout the Gospels: "Who are my mother and my brothers? Those who do the will of God—these are my mother and brothers" and "Woman behold your son. Son, behold your mother" as endorsement of a radical new understanding of kinship.

Through her research, Virginia Ramey Mollenkott has created a list entitled "Diverse Forms of Family Mentioned or Implied in the Hebrew and Christian Scriptures," in which forty different patterns are documented. The options for biblical families range from "Interracial/intercultural marriages" to "Unrelated people traveling with Jesus" to "Families established through incest" and "Childless marriages." "Polygamous marriage," "Patriarchal extended families," and "Female-headed extended families" can be found, as well as "Christian communes" and "An equal-partner, dual-career marriage."[9] By comparison, same-gender loving couples seem fairly tame!

Rosemary Radford Ruether goes further in her critique of family in the New Testament, writing, "The New Testament's negation of the family . . . carries an implicit judgment regarding the family as an expression of worldly power. Moreover, its vision of the church as an alternative family was itself in profound tension with the existing social constructions of the family in the Jewish and Greco-Roman worlds." [10] This struggle over using the family as means of determining status and power has much in common with our struggles today. The efforts of same-gender loving couples to seek equality and freedom from discrimination begs questions of meaning, purpose, and power for all couples and families, engaging us in valuable conversation and discernment.

Finally, these varied and confusing messages about sexuality and family in biblical times are filtered through the multiple messages of our own time and cultures. Just as in the past, today's scholars and researchers are conditioned by their own cultural mores, values, and language. David G. Myers and Letha Dawson Scanzoni point out those translators who have far too often oversimplified words, which in turn obscures the real message. They list thirteen different variations among Bible translations attempting to render multiple Greek constructs into English.

> Some translators simply decided to combine the two Greek words and render them as one, the English word homosexual. They thereby created a host of new problems. Such a translation gave readers the impression that the Bible condemns all homosexual persons, even though homosexual orientation was not being discussed and was not even understood in the modern sense. . . . The word homosexual would imply that women were being discussed, too, even though women were not included in what is described in these original texts.[11]

If Greek scholars cannot agree on what was being conveyed in the original scripts, why do we expect ourselves to get it, or to accept one translation at face value?

All of this points us back to where we started, that is, back to a personal relationship in which we each engage with the words of scripture. We must take responsibility for what we bring to this endeavor, learn the tools we need to take the communal text of our faith seriously, and claim the journey as our own. In so doing, we foster a relationship of spiritual integrity, adding our words of love and struggle to the words of those who have gone before.

AN AFFIRMING AND LIBERATING MESSAGE FOR SAME-GENDER LOVING COUPLES

"Viewed in faith, our sexuality is the Creator's way of calling us out of separation, self-centeredness, and loneliness into communication and communion. It is the grounding of our passion for life, the bodily energy of love."[12]

Christian incarnational theology begins with the significance of the embodiment of God in the human, Jesus, as well as the physicality of our own body-selves within a web of creation. Queer liberation theology starts with the experience of LGBTQ persons and seeks to discover where scripture and theology connect with lived experience. Both of these offer helpful and affirming approaches to the Bible for same-gender loving couples. Combined with biblical scholarship of integrity, these offer significant scriptural themes for the understanding and support of same-gender loving couples.

NOTHING IN CREATION IS SHAMEFUL OR UNCLEAN

The Acts of the Apostles tells the story of Peter's dream, in which he saw a vision from God of a sheet floating down from heaven with numerous types of animals, birds, and reptiles. Peter hears God's voice telling him to kill and eat the animals. Yet Peter, who has kept kosher law, responds that he has never eaten anything unclean. In turn, God rebukes him, "What God has made clean, you must not call profane." After three experiences of this, Peter understands and soon thereafter witnesses the presence of the Holy Spirit in the Gentiles, also believed by the dominant culture to be impure.

Moved by their faith, Peter baptizes them, and sits down to a meal in their household. When scolded by his colleagues for communing with the impure, Peter tells the story, ending with, "If God gave them the same gift that God gave us when we believed in the Lord Jesus Christ, who was I then that I could hinder God?" (Acts 11:17). God's creation, whether of earthly animals or feared and ostracized human others, is never innately bad. In fact, it may become the very place of the manifestation of God's presence. Thus, our natural, created, and embodied longing for sexual and emotional intimacy with our chosen partner of either sex or gender identity is never an occasion of shame and may become the manifestation of God's Holy Spirit.

IMAGES OF SAME-GENDER LOVING COUPLES IN SCRIPTURE

Throughout Hebrew and Christian scriptures one can find recordings of same-sex couples joined together as life companions. While the details of their emotional and sexual intimacy are not recorded, neither are they recorded for heterosexual companions.

The story of Ruth and Naomi is one of deep and abiding commitment between two women journeying together in a risky patriarchal world. Scholars point to the fact that the Hebrew word used to describe Ruth's "clinging" to Naomi is the same word used in Genesis 2:24 to describe the clinging of a man to a woman in marriage.[13] The intimate plea that Ruth speaks to Naomi is one of the most profound and beautiful illustrations of the bond between couples, and it has been used for generations and across cultures in heterosexual wedding ceremonies, often without recognition of its true same-sex relationship context.

> Do not press me to leave you or to turn back from following you! Where you go, I will go; where you lodge, I will lodge; your people shall be my people, and your God my God. Where you die, I will die—there will I be buried. May the Lord do thus and so to me, and more as well, if even death parts me from you! (Ruth 1:16)

One is hard pressed to find a more eloquent description of the covenant between life partners in any language or culture, whatever one's sexual orientation or gender identity.

The abiding relationship between David and Jonathan as recorded in 1 and 2 Samuel provides a beautiful description of love between men. "Your love is more extraordinary to me than the love of women" (2 Sam. 1:26). "Jonathan, son of Saul took great delight in David" (1 Sam. 19:1). Again, we cannot say with surety that their long friendship did or did not include sexual intimacy. Scholars have noted that the language of love at that time included political relationships as well as sexual and emotional intimacy: "terms such as 'love,' which modern readers are inclined to give fixed, universal, and heteronormative meanings, actually are used in very diverse ways under the changing conditions of history and culture."[14] The desolation of David's loss at Jonathan's death and the aimlessness of his later relationships are telling details of the depth of their intimacy.

The relationship between Jesus and the beloved disciple provides yet another example of deep abiding same-sex love. At least five times, the Gospel of John refers to a male disciple as "the one whom Jesus loved." Theodore Jennings asserts that there are several references to this relationship that describe common patterns for life partners: "Nothing is made in the text of the specific form of sexuality that mediates this relationship. . . . At stake here is simply that they were lovers."[15] First of all, he is simply known as Jesus' beloved among the disciples and holds a unique recognized place without special authority or work. There is physical proximity and intimacy between them at the Last Supper, unlike the others. Finally, at the time of his death, Jesus instructs his beloved and his mother to watch over one another, as was the custom for mother and son-in-law at the time. In many ways, this relationship provides a positive role model for same-gender loving couples.

THE SUBVERSION OF GENDER IN SCRIPTURE

The Song of Solomon, long used in same-sex covenanting ceremonies, presents the most overt and beautiful celebration of erotic sensuality and sexuality in the Bible, and perhaps in all literature. Through poetry, the writer voices his love and physical desire for union with the beloved. Christopher King states, "The man falls in love with a chosen outsider, the Shulamite, and their illicit love is expressed fully between equal partners. Their love reflects an ethic of intimacy rather than gender complimentarity."[16]

Many scholars have commented upon the ways in which Jesus and his early followers challenged the accepted roles for women and men within their community. Stories of Jesus associating with women and descriptions of him and the disciples embracing traditionally "feminine" roles, tasks, and ways of being call into questions many unexamined assumptions. These actions provide inspiration for same-gender loving couples to leave behind social norms and customs of gender roles and the need for gender complementarity in relationships. As Theodore Jennings says, "The Jesus tradition affirms the very sort of gender subversion that was sometimes associated with same-sex love."[17]

The story of the Ethiopian eunuch in the book of Acts (8:26–40) serves as another example that the community of faith embraced and was enhanced by those outside gender norms. Considered part of a sexual minority, the Ethiopian eunuch is the first Gentile Christian convert, and he serves as a model of inclusion for all, however we and our partners identify as male and/or female.

Perhaps the point of all of these examples is to be found in Galatians, "In Christ there is neither male nor female" (Gal 3:28). We are welcome as individuals and couples, whatever our sexual orientation and gender identity; and we stand in a long line of those who have challenged social norms before us.

THE NORMATIVE ETHIC OF LOVE IN SCRIPTURE

In addition to the new insights and models offered through a queer reading of biblical texts, same-gender loving couples approach scripture for the same affirmation and direction as heterosexual couples. As theologian Walter Wink writes, "There is no biblical sex ethic. The

Bible knows only a love ethic, which is constantly being brought to bear on whatever sexual mores are dominant in any given country, or culture, or period."[18] The Bible does have a lot to say about the quality of love, but not about imposed social rules restricting who may love whom. Rather, the essence of scripture describes the essence of spiritual and sexual love embodied in the full union of life partners, regardless of sex and gender.

The whole of scripture calls us to relationships of mutuality—mutual respect, mutual caring, and mutual joy. In our intimate partnerships we manifest grateful stewardship for the gifts of creation. As we honor our own and our partner's body-selves, we embrace the incarnation of all that is passionate and holy. In our experience of life-giving intimacy, we find ourselves more deeply connected to God and to our sisters and brothers across the earth. As we care for each other over time, we embody the love of the Holy One for each of us. The Episcopal liturgy for marriage says that people get married for "their mutual joy." May this indeed be so.

3

Horizons: Legal, Cultural, and Religious

Inevitably during the time lapse between the writing, publishing, and reading of this chapter, the legal, cultural, and religious skylines across the environment of same-gender loving couples will look different. Just as shifting clouds and colors reflected in the sun's light draw our attention to first one view and then another, so too, the concerns and issues of same-sex couples and their families are constantly changing. Legislative processes will demand energy and attention—some continuing progress in the rights and recognition of all couples and families, others working to prevent retraction and erosion of such progress. Religious communities will continue to struggle with the call to become more welcoming and affirming of queer people—some advocating tirelessly for the expansion of legal and social justice, many navigating ongoing conflicts about their own responses to the concerns of LGBTQ persons, and others mobilized to maintain heterosexist privilege in all arenas of life. As more gay, lesbian, bisexual, and gender variant people come out, publicly integrating into the daily fabric of society, our common cultural life will be impacted and will continue to change cultures across the world.

Thus, perhaps there are only a few statements we can make with confidence about what lies ahead on the horizon for same-gender loving couples. First, there is no doubt that change will continue to be constant and possibly chaotic. The ground beneath the feet of marriage is moving, with and without the push for legal same-sex marriage. As relationship and family patterns shift and our experience of gender changes, the dynamics and expressions of marriage will continue to evolve. In the words of Stephanie Coontz:

> The revolution in marriage has transformed how people organize their work and personal commitments, use their leisure time, understand their sexuality, and take care of children and the elderly. It has liberated some people from restrictive inherited roles in society. But it has stripped others of traditional support systems and rules of behavior without establishing new ones. . . . This is a recurring pattern in periods of massive historical change.[1]

Along with the social transformation of the institution of marriage, changes in the experiences of same-gender loving couples at home and in society will move and grow. As people navigate changing understandings and expressions of sexuality, dynamics within and around LGBTQ persons from one region of the world to another will interact and impact each other. Accordingly subcultures within all societies will shift.

Second, as the Rev. Dr. Martin Luther King is often quoted, "The arc of the moral universe is long, but it bends towards justice."[2] The human and civil rights of LGBTQ people constitute a moral good, and the movement for justice has arisen from such a groundswell that it is not going to turn around. As is the case with other struggles for justice, there will continue to be setbacks and gains, tears of celebration and sobs of pain. Nonetheless, there is no return to the past of maintaining privilege for some while enforcing oppression for others.

Third, no matter what happens in the near or distant future, same-gender loving couples are not going away. Again, as more come out, it becomes more obvious that LGBTQ people are embedded in the very fabric of all human communities. The early gay and lesbian rights organizing phrase "We Are Everywhere" is true. Thus, congregations, clergy, and spiritual care providers will continue to be called upon for both pastoral care and advocacy needs of LGBTQ people and their families. These occasions will range from the blessing and baptism of children born to same-gender loving couples to the call for testimony at legislative hearings. Consequently, as the needs of the community change and grow, religious leaders will need to learn new tools for pastoral and congregational care.

THE LEGAL HORIZON

As of the spring of 2009, seven countries had legalized same-sex marriage (Belgium, Canada, Netherlands, Norway, South Africa, Spain, and Sweden). Four others had recognized legal same-sex marriages from other countries; fourteen countries had provided legal civil unions and registered partnerships of same-sex couples; numerous others had recognized same-sex civil unions and partnerships in various regions; while still more were involved in debates about the issue.[3] Obviously, the legal status of same-sex couples is in focus and flux throughout our global human community.

The work of legalizing same-sex marriage in the United States is being addressed at local, state and federal levels, with the concentrated effort on addressing state law. As of this writing, a growing minority of states recognize same-sex legal marriage, with similar legislation in process in more. Numerous states have bills pending to either repeal or propose constitutional bans against gay marriage and either extend or limit rights to same-sex partners. Some states currently recognize same-sex marriages from other states, while others prohibit such recognition. Similar or equivalent statewide spousal rights of marriage are offered through civil unions or domestic partnerships and reciprocal beneficiaries.[4] While some of the specifics of the legal data will have changed by the time of this printing, the process and content will continue to be in the forefront of our national agenda.

Although the gains made within several states of the United States in regards to same-sex couples' legal status are significant, the limitations of these gains are also quite obvious. For example, if a couple moves from one state to another, they must consider the effect it has upon their relationship status. Or, if a partner in a legally recognized union/marriage in one state is hospitalized in another state that prohibits same-sex marriage, then his or her partner may not be recognized as next-of-kin. This means that one's partner may not be allowed to visit or make health care decisions during a medical crisis, even though they are married. Currently, the Defense of Marriage Act of 1996 (DOMA) prohibits the federal government from recognizing anything other than opposite sex relationships as legal marriage and allows individual states to refuse recognition of couples from other states. Therefore, whatever state laws may secure for same-gender loving couples has no effect on federal legislation. This prevents partners and some children from receiving social security benefits for which they have been taxed and greatly harms some same-gender loving couples. For example, if one of the partners in a same-sex legal marriage or partnership is a citizen of another country, he or she cannot immigrate to the United States with the partner who is a legal citizen. However, opposite sex married partners can immigrate based solely on their relationship status.

The combination of DOMA and the "Don't ask, don't tell" policy of the military prevents same-sex partners of military personnel from many rights—even that of being informed in case of illness or death. In sum, there are over 1,100 rights, benefits, and responsibilities conferred on married couples by the federal government, including access to health care, parenting and immigration rights, social security, veterans and survivor benefits, and transfer of property—and that doesn't include those conferred by state and local law, practices of employer, or the intangible security, dignity, and meaning that comes with marriage.[5] Both DOMA and the military's "Don't ask, don't tell" policy are on the table for reconsideration and possible revocation.

Another interesting dynamic on the legal marriage front has emerged with the coming out of transsexual individuals and their partners. Specifically, if legal marriage is based upon gender/sex, and one of the partners changes legal sex and gender identity, then what happens to the marriage? Across the country in states that prohibit same-sex marriage, same-gender loving couples are, in fact, legally married. How has this happened? A genetic male and female marry one another. Then, at some point in the marriage, one partner comes out as transsexual, proceeds through the medical treatment protocol, resulting in the legal change of sex. Thus, the same couple that was one man and one woman is now two women or two men, and is still legally married. Perhaps one of the gifts that transgender and transsexual persons offer is a clear example of the futility of clinging to socially constructed categories of gender and sex in our legal and cultural understanding of love and marriage.

THE CULTURAL HORIZON

It seems that no matter how much negative press marriage receives, no matter how high the divorce rate soars or how often comedians and cynics poke fun at "'til death do us part," no matter how confused we may all be about ceremonial customs and rituals or how we may struggle to find language that actually works to describe relationships, we still love marriage and weddings. With our current cultural emphasis on love and personal choice, marriages now hold more potential for joy, justice, and long-term companionship than they did in the past. In our society, legal marriage no longer serves political alliances or defines one person as property of another. The home is no longer considered off limits to laws protecting family members from violence and abuse. Whether gay or straight, modern marriage offers both partners a vision of mutuality, equality, and individual respect. Marriage is about relational fulfillment and abiding commitment. At the same time, it is not the only option for lifetime companionship and commitment. Modern marriage is no longer a requirement of adulthood. It is a cultural choice.

In her groundbreaking gay rights book *Virtual Equality*, Irvashi Vaid writes of the importance of cultural change alongside legal changes in the quest for justice for LGBTQ people. Citing research that most people who are hostile to gay and lesbian people have limited contact with them, she writes convincingly of the need to come out. Most people change their false beliefs about queer people through personal contact. Cultural change only happens when LGBTQ people come out in every walk of life, so that neighbors, coworkers, family members, and religious congregations can no longer pretend that queer people are not in their midst, embedded in their everyday lives. She also says, "Homosexuality always involves choice—indeed, it involves a series of four major choices: admitting, acting, telling, and living . . . being openly gay allows us to develop strong, unashamed, and whole selves."[6]

In the last several years many same-gender loving couples and their families have chosen to come out, to tell the story of their lived lives, creating permanent and irreversible changes in our cultural beliefs about marriage and family.

As long as same-gender loving couples, whether gay, lesbian, or transgender, continue to come out across the many and varied communities of our nation and world, the work for marriage equality will move forward. LGBTQ people are changing marriage, and marriage is changing them. Laurie Israel is an attorney in Massachusetts and a married lesbian. In an article entitled "Marriage: The Final Frontier," she writes:

> So what can straight people teach gays and lesbians about marriage? That it . . . promotes personal growth, family connections, psychological health, and financial security . . . that even if your marriage isn't perfect . . . it is ultimately worthwhile . . . that lifetime relationships with no end until death are extremely valuable, even if achieved at some hard costs. And what can gays and lesbians teach straight people about marriage? That marriage is precious . . . that marriage should be cherished, savored, and protected . . . always appreciate that you have the opportunity to be married.[7]

Even though there may be strongly held differences of opinion about marriage and family, it is impossible not to agree that our common cultural experiences are in a sea of change. It can feel as if we are together in a small boat, riding atop a big wave, unsure of who's in charge and where we might land. Nonetheless, we are surfing together, and we will land somewhere. Family sociologist and demographer Susan Stewart, PhD, offers a helpful image to understand the complexities of these changes by suggesting that we are living in a "mosaic" of family patterns.[8] Every mosaic is a work of art, made more beautiful by each color and design weaving in, out, and among the others. So, too, may our culture celebrate the intricate patterns and multiple designs of love and commitment, honoring diversity in the meaning and expression of family and cherishing the partnerships of all who chose to love.

THE RELIGIOUS HORIZON

No discussion of the current and future trends in the relationship of religion and same-gender loving couples can occur in isolation. We live in a time of great religious diversity. Most of us are more aware of religious pluralism than ever, and of the importance of engaging in multifaith conversations. There are some specific concerns and dynamics of which religious leaders and same-gender loving couples need to ask: Why is it that sexuality in general and sexual orientation in particular are such "hot-button "issues in religion? Why are there such deeply emotional conflicts within individual Christian denominations and across the spectrum of Christianity as well as within other major religions? Why does sexuality seem to be such a dividing line in a lot of multifaith and multicultural communication? These are critical questions for people of faith to explore if we are to live together in human community.

Although there is no way to fully address these concerns in this chapter, it is important to realize that sexuality is at the same time an intimate and a public aspect of our human experience. It encompasses what is most personal and private to us while at the same time serving what is most communal in the building of relations based on gender and family structures. Sexuality has served as a primary arena of power and control in most societies and religions. The regulation of family patterns, sexual practices, and gender expression and roles has established and maintained cultural and economic hegemony by some, at the expense of others. Even in a country that values the separation of church and state, much of this regulation has been grounded in the traditions of the Christian church.

> These quintessential American assumptions about religion, values, and public life are crucially connected to sexuality and its regulation . . . concerning homosexuality, the Court refers directly to Christian religious tradition to support its position. . . . Why does religion seem like the natural and appropriate basis for public policy concerning sex, but not for the other ethically charge questions? Poverty, the death penalty, the exploitation of the earth's resources. . . . Why do assumptions change when it comes to sex? . . . because time after time and issue after issue, it seems that sexual matters become the measures of an individual's—and even a nation's—overall morality.[9]

What is important on the horizon for same-gender loving couples is the realization that they have become a kind of lightening rod, litmus test, and red herring all at the same time. In the present-day struggles of religion and civic life, homosexuality and gay marriage seem to define who we are and where we stand—either drawing us together or pulling us apart. The work of liberation and justice for some has become the demarcation of difference and limitation for others. Religious leaders and people of faith need to understand the importance of religion and public life, and the interconnections between sexuality and religion, if we are to foster healthy dialogue and justice for those who have been oppressed.

There is obvious work here in the realm of religion and public life; however, there is also personal work for couples and providers of pastoral care.

As more same-gender loving couples and their families come out, fully integrating into religious communities, the movement towards full marriage equality will be strengthened. Denominational and congregational leadership will need to continue to address the concerns and conflicts surrounding sexuality and same-sex marriage—hopefully providing leadership for justice and equality, and care for those in our midst. In the words of James Nelson, our churches need to be moving away from a kind of "Family Fundamentalism" into a rich celebration of family diversity in its many expressions.

At the same time, the specific pastoral care needs of same-gender loving couples and their families need to be addressed with skill and knowledge. Certainly, gay, lesbian, bisexual, and transgender couples share many of the basic concerns and needs for care that heterosexual couples have. However, life as a lightening rod, litmus test, and red herring takes its toll. The particular stresses and strains of LGBTQ couples and families need to be tended to, along with the joys and celebrations of gains made.

In summary, the horizon looks busy. A lot of shifts and changes, demands and growing responsibilities will gather across the skyline, sometimes culminating into torrential downpours and other times in a gorgeous sunrise. Let us remain watchful and alert so that we may actively participate in the creation of a world of beauty.

Part Two

From the Clergy Perspective

Introduction

Improvisation on Sonnet CXVI

for Regina and Sara

Then let us not impede with narrow minds
these two women who more than twenty years
have altered not in love, in care, in kind—
smiling for joy and sharing deepest tears.
O No. Now may New Hampshire clearly state—
it is a state where they may vow and dance,
as well as those who have no cause to wait,
and with the future's suns and tempests chance.
For woman with woman, man with man shall love
in days of rosy cheeks or creased with age,
as true as neighbors never asked to prove
their tenderness upon the world's bright stage.

My sonnet improvise a sweet caressing—
Shakespeare, law and God this day give blessing.

I dedicate my part of this book to three and a half couples. I dedicate this book to Regina and Sara, who were the first same-gender loving couple for whom I performed a legal civil union in my own state—

New Hampshire—on March 29, 2008. It was fun, it was festive, it was musical, it was tender, there were (were there really?) ten young people involved (am I crazy?) and it was lawful. That is not just a difference for the couple—it is a difference for a clergyperson.

I also dedicate this work to Neil and Carol Ann, whom I married May 2, 1992. It was the fifty-eighth wedding I had performed. They were the first heterosexual couple who asked me to insert into their wedding a prayer that would acknowledge and affirm the gay and lesbian guests who would be at their wedding. The prayer began like this:

> O God, gentle and wondrous Shepherd of all people, who blesses the lives of men and women, young and old, a magnificent diversity of race and cultures and traditions and sexual orientations, we give you thanks that you accompany each of us in our journeys through life—through joy and sorrow, in times of wonder, doubt, or pain, at moments of birth and death. We praise you that in the journey individuals become attracted in unique and deeply meaningful ways and risk making commitments to one another. Today we rejoice in the covenant of marriage and its particular pleasures of physical, emotional, and spiritual embrace . . .

My words became more eloquent and bolder as the years of weddings went on. I never placed a prayer that broadened the definition of covenantal relationship into a couple's wedding without asking them, but also I never failed to ask a couple if they would like such a prayer included. Because of Carol and Neil, many couples at the moment of their joy have considered the intolerance experienced by others and the possibility of making their own celebration an opportunity for verbal hospitality. About half choose to include such a prayer. And as a clergyperson I think about it—not only when I am meeting with same-gender loving couples, but as widening the understanding of love for every couple.

I dedicate this work to N. and S., the first same-gender loving couple I married who later divorced. How I idealized gay and lesbian marriages! How I cheated them of the right to be human! Intolerance wears a number of masks. Thanks to N. and S., I don't assume all same-gender loving couples who have been in a relationship for a long time want to be married; I don't assume that all couples will succeed in marriage; I don't assume all couples have been hurt by the church or are rejected by some members of their families. I don't even assume they know what they are doing!

Finally I dedicate this work to Donald Tirabassi, the other half of my couple, with whom I know the inside of love and longing, of partnering and parenting, with whom I know what it is to want and leap into and occasionally regret marriage, and with whom I know anniversaries. Weddings are great. The real purpose of this book is to provide the context for people to have anniversaries! (And health benefits, custody rights, funeral choices, hospital visitation, and tax and property simplicity—if that can ever be!)

All people should have the right to marriage with its blessings and boredoms and the right to such matter of fact anniversaries that every once in a while one of them will be forgotten. And for that I celebrate being an LGBTQ ally. I do not have a child or a sibling or a parent who is gay or lesbian. The people in my life who are same-gender loving are chosen family. One member of one search committee asked me, "Well, what's the motivation for your intensity about this issue?" "Jesus Christ."

Being an LGBTQ ally has been the lynchpin of my ministry from the moment in 1978 when I was prepared for ordination and discovered that suddenly my denomination was not going to allow gay and lesbian people to be ordained and I needed to walk away from it and find another denomination in which to prepare for my commitment. It has been the reason I've been called to churches and sometimes the reason my candidacy has been . . . discouraged. If sacred and/or civil marriages, unions, and covenants of same-gender loving couples are ministered to only by gay, lesbian, bisexual, and transgender clergy, then a new form of ghetto will be created. We now turn in this book to theoretical and practical elements of marriage preparation, to congregational and community conflict and conversation, to family relationships, the rhythms of rehearsals, and the sweet words of vows. This section is for clergy, all clergy. Loosen your collar (whatever kind you wear), light the parsonage fire, set aside the sermon notes and the deacons' agenda. Consider your ministry year in and year out with couples in the celebration that scripture claims is modeled on Christ's love for the community of God's people.

—Maren C. Tirabassi

4

Precovenanting Conversations and Pastoral Care Tools

A Prayer of Preparation

for use by a pastor preparing to meet with a longtime couple

Holy Spirit, dwelling within me,
give me an open mind and heart,
as I meet with these two people who seek your blessing
upon their faithful commitment of many years.
May I listen deeply and discern clearly
the ways that, through them, you invite me
into deeper understanding of your love and grace
for all creation.

Allow me, I pray,
to witness the ways you have been at work in each of them
and in their unfolding relationship.
May I be an honest and faithful companion to them on their
spiritual journey.
Help me understand the ways you may be calling me
to be a force for healing and reconciliation
in their lives individually and as a couple.
May I be an instrument of your peace, justice, and grace,
instilling hope and love where possible.

O God, guide me
to understand and reflect the hopes, dreams, and desires of this couple
that have already been realized
and that long for further deepening and development
in your holy wisdom.
May I understand, affirm, and bless the ways this couple
has already and will continue to
reflect your own yearning—your hopes, dreams, and desires
for furthering love and justice, hope and mercy, forgiveness and
 reconciliation
in them and in the world.

I pray all of this in the name of Jesus,
our brother and savior, Amen.

The Rev. Dr. Kenneth Orth[1]

Clergy have strong opinions about weddings! Joining in the celebration of community and family, sharing in the joy and excitement of love, and engaging hope with an eye to the future, some ministers love to officiate for couples at this juncture in life. Others dread weddings, thinking of them as a necessary part of the job and something that takes them away from their own leisure on beautiful Saturday afternoons. Why such strong feelings? Perhaps as marriage has changed, so have weddings. The culture of western, white heterosexual weddings has become one of performance and show, often breaking the bank to fund, and more often than not ending in divorce court. How many couples come to their minister first, and only afterwards put up the deposit for the reception hall? How many drive around town looking for a pretty church building or the perfect destination, then "hire" the minister to get it done? It can feel to pastors like we are more easily replaced than caterers and often less personally significant to the couple. And yet, something new is happening. The rising tide of same-gender loving couples seeking legal and nonlegal religious ceremonies of covenant provides something new and exciting for clergy. Specifically, we are being called to a new accountability and opportunity to reconsider our pastoral role with individuals as they join together in unions of justice-love. As couples come to us for blessing and the authority and skills implied in our profession, we are held to a standard of theological hope-in-relation, and ministerial competence in pastoral care and worship. In addition, we are being offered the opportunity to engage in an expanding and deepening process of creative liturgical renewal and honest pastoral conversations with couples.

In the book *Becoming Married*, Herbert Anderson and Robert Fite describe three pastoral roles in prewedding work. First, we serve as a "friend" to the couple, in the sense that we welcome them into the space of a healthy pastoral relationship without personal agenda. Couples are constantly navigating other peoples' expectations and opinions, especially those of family and friends. Therefore, the offer of hospitality that honors the relationship, listens nonjudgmentally to worry and doubt, and enables discernment of strengths and shortcomings, hopes and dreams is vitally significant to any couple in the journey of covenanting love.

Second, the pastor also serves as "teacher" with couples. Preparation for a wedding/covenanting ceremony provides a rare window of opportunity to engage couples' reflections on a number of significant issues in their life together. We can foster learning and preparedness for a lifetime of love much as we foster thoughtful expression and experience of the service itself. "Because of our emphasis on the significance of the wedding itself, we stress the importance of catechesis in the traditional sense as preparation for liturgy. Education for marriage is an important agenda for the churches' ministry to couples."[2]

Finally, we are called to advocate for the couple in our work for relational health in both the couple and each individual partner. Sometimes this means that we try to move them into a deeper understanding and embodiment of loving mutuality. At other times, we may work to increase firmer boundaries with unhealthy or unsupportive families of origin. Still further, we may be advocating for the liberation of couples from false cultural projections and internalized scripts of harm to their religious, emotional, and social well-being. Each of these pastoral roles revitalizes the possibilities for pastors to deepen the integrity of care and relational justice. Again in the words of Anderson and Fife:

> We begin with human experience and move from there to the tradition of faith regarding the significance of marriage. The pastoral task is to help couples move from their own stories and their own values and dreams for their life together, however vaguely religious they might be, to the Christian tradition in order to deepen and expand their vision. To be able to blend liturgical and theological expertise into a process that is truly collaborative is a highly developed pastoral art.[3]

Historically, the heterosexual wedding ceremony has served as a rite of passage occurring through a series of rituals. This rite of passage has emphasized the transitional process of separation from one's family of origin, individuation, and then reintegration into a new family identity. Even with the many changes surrounding heterosexual coupling in our culture, these themes continue to be present. However, in LGBTQ couples, these rituals and themes are not often present or may have a different spin to them.

For example, instead of integrating a new family identity, the ceremony may solidify a community identity. Many times, same-gender loving couples have long ago worked through the adult transitional stages and have clear identities of themselves as individuals and couples. Depending upon the social location and public acknowledgement of the couple as "family," the individual identity may be more internalized and integrated than the couple identity. In states where same-gender loving marriage or civil unions are legally recognized, LGBTQ couples have ceremonies for many of the same reasons that heterosexual couples do. Specifically, couples seek the legal and social status and recognition conferred upon them by civil and religious ceremonies. In states that do not recognize same-sex legal marriage or civil unions, many LGBTQ couples also seek covenanting ceremonies, but for different reasons. Primarily, these reasons speak to the importance of receiving public validation and support for their relationship and ritualizing the commitment between the individuals in a couple. Often, same-gender loving covenanting ceremonies do not begin a process of transition, and are often not new commitments. On the other hand, they do often crystallize/confer public support (with or without family support). They also provide role modeling and function as political acts of resistance to religious and social homophobia.

After researching several same-gender loving couples who had held public ceremonies that they called "weddings," "unions," or "commitment ceremonies," Gretchen Stiers writes:

> Like heterosexuals, lesbians and gay men clearly have ceremonies because they love their partners and want to acknowledge that bond publicly. Indeed, like heterosexual weddings, lesbian and gay ceremonies serve to integrate a couple into larger kinship and community networks. At their core same-sex ceremonies are rites of integration as well as rites of passage; their two primary objectives are the creation of family and the building of community.[4]

Therefore, many of the issues in premarital counseling of heterosexual couples are relevant to same-gender loving couples. However, there are also specific dynamics of LGBTQ coupling that need attention. A new factor of which we should be cognizant comes as a result of the groundswell of the movement for marriage equality. Ironically, some same-gender loving couples may feel social pressure to "get married" in order to do their part for the community, even if their relationship is not ready or appropriate for this very personal step. Others find that the legalization of civil unions or marriage destabilizes the relational dynamic that had worked for years, thereby creating conflict where there had been none. After civil unions became legal in their state, one gay male couple that had been together for more than three decades discovered that they held different ideas about their relationship. Assuming that they would be one of the first couples to sign on, one partner excitedly began making plans for the ceremony. The other partner described himself as having "cold feet," realizing that the nonlegal status of their relationship had given him an "escape hatch" all these years.

Even though they had a wonderful relationship that he had never left nor ever wanted to, he had internalized the cultural message that gay relationships don't last, and that he could leave anytime. The possibility of a civil union suddenly pushed them into a process of naming and navigating unknown conflicts.

Finally, it is critical that pastors bring a multicultural perspective to our work with all couples, realizing that cultural messages and meanings about sexuality, family, and marriage can differ greatly.[5] Facilitating partners' mutual exploration of the impact of the race/ethnicity of their family of origin, and the cultural narratives about sexual orientation, gender identity/expression, family bonds, and beliefs about marriage is key to the advocacy of care to which we are called. Often couples are not aware of the many layers of internalized scripts about same-gender loving couples, their similarities and differences with heterosexual partnerships, or the interplay between them. Thus, it is important for the pastor to be alert to the possibilities of raising these within the context of premarital/covenantal counseling.

SPECIFIC ISSUES FOR PASTORAL CONVERSATIONS

Compatibility of Coming Out History and Openness

One's history of coming to terms with and joyfully claiming one's sexual identity is a crucial factor in self-understanding and the ability to be intimate. These are important stories to be woven into the couples' identity and shared narrative. Of even greater significance is the discernment of comfort with being out as a couple. For example, if one partner is committed to being out to everyone she/he encounters, while the other partner is closeted to her/his family of origin, there is a built-in conflict. Relationships have ended over these issues. In educational forums, GLAD (Gay and Lesbian Advocates and Defenders) representatives stress that once a couple is legally joined in civil union or marriage, then neither partner can remain closeted in any way. In other words, one cannot lie about legal matters. Couples must be aware of this. It is equally important for the pastor to help the couple talk about and come to agreement on how they present themselves to family, friends, and community. All research concludes that the more out and less secretive someone is about his/her sexual orientation, the more emotionally and spiritually healthy he/she can be. This is also true with couples.

Family of Origin Relationships and Support

Family relationships and support are important for all couples. However, they are often more complex and conflicted for same-gender loving couples. Sometimes one or the other partner's family is less than supportive. It is important to help the couple talk about this, affirm what can be affirmed, grieve what must be grieved, and set realistic goals for family connections. There are times when family members hold on to their refusal to be present at the ceremony, believing that attendance expresses full support and runs counter to their beliefs. Other times, family members will attend even if they are conflicted in their religious and social perspectives. This has proven to be a healing moment in the life of some, loosening tightly held beliefs and deepening the bond of family.

> For a small minority of respondents, however, having a ceremony altered the meaning of family for some of their biological relatives. In particular, attending a same-sex ceremony changed how some parents understood their daughter's or son's sexual identity as well as the nature of their relationship. Although most lesbian and gay couples do not "consciously" decide to have a ceremony for this reason, the ceremony itself may change how they are accepted and included in their biological families.[6]

If someone's family of origin is particularly homophobic or negative, it can be helpful to speak about the couple's "family of choice" as a way to empower the couple to seek and affirm close family-like bonds with others. Finally, it is important that same-gender loving couples do not take on the heterosexist projections of family members. Though there are similarities, LGBTQ couples are not just like heterosexual couples, nor are they different in ways of cultural stereotypes. Therefore, each couple needs to be aware and assess whatever gendered family traditions they wish to embrace or discard, perhaps using this as a teaching moment for family members.

Community support

Although this is something that many heterosexual couples have the luxury of taking for granted, many same-gender loving couples need to be intentional about it. One cannot assume support in the same way. Creating community through church, social networks, advocacy organizations, neighborhoods, and more provides a critical component to the long-term foundation for every couple. Thus, it is helpful to speak with a couple about the places they might be assured of community support and to ritualize/affirm them in the ceremony.

Legal, Medical, Financial Planning

At the time of legal marriage and civil unions, significant (yet limited) rights and responsibilities are immediately conferred upon the couple. However, this is not at all true with nonlegal ceremonies. Therefore, it is imperative that the couple does all they can to protect themselves. Too often couples are hesitant to do this. It is not pleasant to talk about death and illness.

However, it is part of the responsibility of healthy coupling. Without appropriate planning a partner might not be allowed in the hospital room or have the right to the body of a deceased nonlegal spouse. One could be forced to move out of one's home while waiting for the will to be executed. It is critical that a pastor be well acquainted with these issues, perhaps having legal/medical referrals for couples. Even in states that recognize same-sex legal marriage or civil unions, the rights of these couples may be limited only to the state of residence or other countries with similar legal protections. Thus, all same-gender loving couples that plan on traveling need to address these concerns. Additionally, not all couples understand the difference between state and federal benefits. After all, there are more than one thousand legal benefits associated with federal marriage that have nothing to do with state law. Therefore, knowing the details of legal benefits and limitations regarding same-gender couples that vary from state to state is a challenge. It is imperative that couples understand what is and is not protected by the state law in which they live.

Monogamy, Safer Sex, and HIV Status

Monogamy is something that we often take for granted; however, it is important to talk openly and honestly about each partner's commitment to and understanding of it in preparation for the taking of relationship vows. For some couples, emotional fidelity and sexual monogamy are not one and the same. Exploring with couples their beliefs about sexual and emotional monogamy and their hopes for the relationship becomes a key ingredient to the making of vows that are both honest and relevant for the days and years to come. It is also important to help the couple agree to compatible safer sex practices within their sexual relationship, as part of discussing sex and sexuality in long-term loving relationships. When partners have a different HIV status, this can cause some concern and fear. Again, helping the couple to talk about this with each other is an important step in fostering emotional and sexual intimacy.

Planning for Children

The options for same-gender loving couples to have and raise children are much broader than they were a few years ago. Thus, many LGBTQ couples include having children as a significant part of their hope for the relationship. Other couples may have at least one partner who is already parenting and brings one or more children into this present relationship. Exploring goals and possibilities for parenting is as critical with same-gender couples as it is with heterosexual couples and, therefore, needs to be a point of discussion in the preparation for covenanted couple life. Just as with heterosexual couples, widely differing assumptions about children can create significant conflict and challenges, as well as joys and celebrations. It is much better to address this at this juncture, rather than wait until a crisis begs discussion.

Religious History/ Spiritual Compatibility/ Church Involvement

All couples need to come to a place of mutual spiritual support for one another, even if their individual needs and beliefs are quite different. Presumably, if a couple has come to a pastor for this work, then there has been some discussion of religion, but not necessarily. With LGBTQ couples, it is important to provide the opportunity to uncover the messages they have gotten from religion about sexual orientation/gender identity, and the impact of those messages upon them. This is also an important opportunity to connect couples with the Welcoming Congregation movement at local and denominational levels.

In his book *The Minister as Diagnostician*, Paul Pruyser lists seven theological themes in pastoral care,[7] which can easily be adapted and explored with same-gender loving couples. These themes are:

1. ***Awareness of the Holy:*** what is sacred to the couple? What inspires awe in them individually and together?
2. ***Providence:*** What are their views of the world—dangerous and unpredictable or safe and secure? What are their views of God—loving, forgiving, demanding, or dismissive?
3. ***Faith:*** In whom/what do they trust? To whom do they turn in times of personal or relationship difficulty?
4. ***Grace or gratefulness:*** When do they share moments of gratitude in their life together? For what are they grateful?
5. ***Sin, repentance, forgiveness:*** What is their understanding of sin and guilt? Are they capable of recognizing and taking responsibility for their own mistakes? Do they take on too much responsibility, or responsibility for others? Do they see themselves as victims of social or personal sin? Can they forgive and let go of resentments?
6. ***Communion (or community):*** How are they engaged as individuals and a couple with others?
7. ***Sense of vocation or purpose:*** How do they understand their reason for being? How do they express a sense of purpose as a couple?

Through the explorations of these themes and the discussion of religious experiences and current connections to community, these conversations can create significant opportunities to deepen a couple's grounding in faith, while opening them to increasing depth and growth in the future.

5

Precovenanting Conversations and Ceremony Preparation

One way clergy can bless same-gender loving couples as they prepare for a ceremony is by helping them simplify the event. The wedding business has grown gluttonous in our culture, frequently impoverishing couples, often putting so much emotional strain on a relationship that only a strong marriage will survive the wedding. For vendors of clothing, cakes, music, facilities, printing services, photography, etc. etc. etc. the excited same-gender loving couple newly able to marry is particularly vulnerable. A second common experience results from the long, impatient wait of some couples. Years of wedding fantasies sometimes result in a cluttered ceremony. The clergyperson may not be able to intervene with overgrown receptions but certainly should bring pruning shears to the ceremony with seven poems, three kinds of promises/vows, two blessings ceremonies (either one of which would be deeply moving), speeches/guitar solos by six important supporters and a miscellany of ribbons, seeds from the garden, and PowerPoint presentations.

Enough! (But "enough" kindly.) The couple rarely has perspective. Indiscriminant inclusions make a beautiful ceremony more like a talent show. Help them focus on the vow. The couple and God should be "stage center."

Here are two suggestions for precovenanting conversations that focus on simplifying. Invite a couple who are involved in church and have some understanding of scripture to read Luke 10:38–42, Jesus' interaction with the two faithful sisters Martha and Mary. This scripture is often read as a personality inventory in miniature (am I a Martha or a Mary?). A clearer interpretation is to ask what it teaches about behaviors at any deeply significant event—the visit of Jesus of Nazareth or the occasion of a lifelong commitment. The couple can reflect on the "one thing needed." Other ancient authorities have "a few things." How can they cut down on distractions, work and worry, and treasure the "better part?"

For the couple typically called "unchurched" and less likely to crack open a Bible, a precovenanting conversation gambit is the question "What's bad and good about Valentine's Day?" What is good, in fact, wonderful, is the story—a collage of several stories—of a priest who was willing to die in order to perform illegal weddings. That commitment to facilitate love in the face of political authority and social pressure is precious.

What's bad about Valentine's Day is the modern vulgar overconsumption of chocolate, flowers, jewelry, and heart-shaped anything, and the cultural identification of "loser" that marks everyone without a romantic involvement as the holiday rolls around. After discussing this contrast, the couple considers how to express the true, and often hard-won, sense of their relationship and discard the cute, the overly sentimental, and the unnecessary wedding expectations.

After simplifying, it is time to stress the importance of community to the ceremony. A wedding or holy union is a choice to make sacred promises in a gathering of witnesses. There is a balance involved—the community is not there to be "pleased," but it needs to be included. Once I was planning a wedding for a couple in a national park, and they wanted to have their vows exchanged on the very ledge where they sat in the rays of sunset and first verbalized their love. Unfortunately, one of the partners had a brother who traveled in a wheelchair. The conversation went like this:

"He could wait at the trailhead."

"You mean your brother will sit alone as the night closes in while the rest of the wedding party celebrates five hundred feet away."

"Ah . . . yes."

"What's wrong with this picture—You two have been on the outside, in the dark, considered dis-abled for marriage, and you are going to allow your wedding to be an occasion for someone else to experience exclusion and isolation?"

Of course, they chose a much more accessible location in the park where kids were safe, older folks could open up folding chairs, the wheelchair easily rolled in and everyone stayed much longer chatting and offering congratulations. On the evening before the wedding—after the rehearsal and before a rehearsal party—the couple climbed with me to the ledge and we had an evening prayer of blessing (see page 169).

There is a balance between inclusion of supportive family and friends and the temptation to try to change the ceremony in order to accommodate unsupportive relatives. The brother-in-law who wants the word "marriage" removed? Ignore him! It is the clergyperson's role to authorize doing just that. Adaptations should not change those parts of the ceremony that are deeply meaningful to the couple.

The sacrament of Holy Communion is a special instance of this issue that applies to all covenanting ceremonies. Every couple should look at their guest list, identifying the faithful of other world religions, of more restrictive Christian denominations, or those who are secular. Shared prayers, witnessed vows, and scripture readings can be more universally experienced than the tangible, tasty, scented embodiment of the Word. Because Eucharist is so powerful, it is a wonderful part of a ceremony, but because it is so powerful it can be divisive. Bishop Jonathan Blake's ceremony for sharing wine and sharing honey (pages 143–44) is one sensual but less combative alternative. Simply passing the peace, so that those gathered shake one another's hands and greet one another rather than only relating to those in a receiving line, engages everyone in incarnation.

"I love you because . . ." is not a vow. Donna Schaper has a delightful printed statement for couples that plan to write portions of their own ceremonies:

Invitation to Write Your Service

Many people like to write their own wedding services. They are eager for the self-expression that implies. Writing sometimes helps us know what we really think, also—it is not just for public consumption. The act of writing our own service, or parts of it, allows us to become articulate about our deepest desires in our largest moment. This eagerness is both noble and difficult! Getting our words right, even in the glorious time before the service, is not easy. Love gets overused. Respect gets overused. Beautiful gets overused. Our task is to find smaller words and stories and details to carry these larger feelings. Again, it is not easy, as any writer will tell you. . . . What is a writer? One who avoids using clichés in order to say something universal and splendid *which has been said before.*[1]

It is a wonderful thing to invite couples to participate in the shaping of their own ceremonies. It is, however, extraordinarily difficult to tell them later that they have done it wrong. And, quite honestly, it is a lot more work and takes much longer to help people write their own than simply to offer them a choice of two or three well-prepared services that say the right things in beautiful words. Nevertheless, the activity itself—whether the words are used in full, excerpted, or paraphrased—is an important tool in the precovenanting conversation that may uncover new depths to the relationship.

A few guidelines are helpful:

First ask the couple, "Are there portions of your ceremony you would like to write?" This implies that they are welcome, but not expected, to contribute and that the clergyperson will definitely do the assembling.

Second, if they want to write part of their ceremony, it will be helpful for you to offer them samples of services so they can follow the format. It is best not to ask them whether they want the assistance, since they might refuse it. People frequently feel that they have been at enough covenanting services (or seen enough movies about weddings . . . and possibly even *I Now Pronounce You Chuck and Larry*) to understand the structure, but that is rarely the case. Without direct assistance, they will head for the Internet, a source of some lovely liturgy, much rubbish, and some materials that the officiant may not wish to verbalize, such as gender exclusive language for God.

"Let me just share a few common pitfalls" is a gracious way to introduce instruction on writing vows, which is the most meaningful and problematic portion of the ceremony. People do not have experience with vow-language in other aspects of contemporary life, so it frequently comes out more like toast-language. In fact, the toast is a tactful place to relocate some statements. It is best to say directly that vows are promises that should mirror each other. A "vow preface" might be unique to each partner, but the vows themselves should always be parallel.

A second pitfall is locating vows too early in the service. Dramatically speaking, they should be near the end. Some couples need help sorting out the statement of intentions from the vows. Finally, a statement of support by all family present or family and friends is a great improvement over "give away" or "accompany" language.

Some of these issues are common to covenanting ceremonies in general and should not need special mention here. However, several factors contribute to clergy ineptitude in preparing for the weddings and unions of same-gender loving couples. Most clergy are so enthusiastic about the opportunity to share this celebration with old parishioners or new friends who may become parishioners in a church open to their ceremony that they become overly sensitive, concerned, tactful. They are also hesitant to be critical with couples who have already faced so much criticism. Finally, many same-gender loving couples have been together for a long time, perhaps longer than the clergyperson has been in ministry. However, it is not the case that a long shared history gives any expertise in wedding liturgy. In fact, that long history is more likely to result in the ceremony clutter mentioned above.

Precovenanting conversations are full of opportunities and responsibilities to improvise. Clergy find themselves offering opinions on flowers, fruit bowls, formal attire, and fussy family. This may be particularly important for same-gender loving couples because a clergyperson may be uniquely neither a vendor nor a close friend. The reflection of an impartial observer is often rare and always a blessing.

One practical suggestion is "five crazy questions." Hand each of the partners five index cards and invite them to write a question on each card about any aspect of the wedding or union ceremony or about the marriage or partnership. If the questions are a homework assignment, they may be more profound, but if they are done in the office or living room, they may be more immediate and raw. Both strategies have advantages. Note first the questions that are the same for both members of the couple. Then work through all the questions, alternating your comments, their thoughts, and your reflection back to them of the decisions they are actually making. This is a wonderful way to defuse free-floating anxiety.

Another practical assistance is to offer to role-play a situation. Volunteer to impersonate a difficult relative, an ex-spouse who is barring the participation of a son or daughter in the ceremony, an old friend, an employer, or a caterer. Set a timer for five minutes and do not break out of character. The purpose is to prepare the person for the real interview. This is a wonderful exercise with either partner, but it also can be a three-way conversation.

"It was the best of times, it was the worst of times." Charles Dickens must have been thinking about a rehearsal. I think I remember a guillotine in that book.

A rehearsal is important for the sake of rehearsing. It is not the "preparty" or the "other family's party." In reality, one can comfort couples by noting that the rehearsal evening is often a magnet for bad behavior. It is not usually a portent of the day to come. People get pettiness out of their systems. There are some general rehearsal rules. Everyone involved should be present. If someone is unavoidably detained, someone besides the couple or the clergy should take responsibility to pass on information. Never wait longer than half an hour! Begin with the ceremony itself and go through every single word with those who are standing in position and paying attention. Only then turn to stage movement"—processional, recessional, circles, seating of the gathered people. This can be repeated until it is comfortable. Finally, discuss logistics, such as the preseating of family, photograph policy, time to arrive, how guests are ushered out or cluster in, the whether and where and who of a receiving line, etc.

The rehearsal is the opportunity for change—in fact, the last opportunity—but it is a good clergy policy to limit suggestions to the couple themselves and stifle the comments of others, so that they do not experience critique about any aspect of the ceremony they have planned. The rehearsal is also a time when the last worries surface about difficult relatives and family strain. Some worries may have been repressed throughout the entire wedding planning process. The officiant is the official improviser, the one who offers to make phone calls or directive suggestions, such as "if your cousin's wife makes openly hostile remarks about gay people when she drinks, maybe she shouldn't come." Many couples are accommodating to a fault!

The rehearsal is also an opportunity for a very personal prayer of blessing—on the couple and those who are the special supportive friends involved in the service. Some of these people may be quite secular. They will still feel honored to be included in the prayer of someone who is officiating for a same-gender loving couple.

Every once in a great while, a couple decides at the last moment not to go through with the wedding or civil union. Their instinct is to send a clergyperson out the door with embarrassed thanks for the time spent. However, often clergy can provide practical assistance in dismantling plans and pastoral care in the loss and alienation of the experience.

This and the preceeding chapter about precovenanting conversations from the clergy perspective are logically attached to "Unique Conversations for Same-Gender Loving Couples" (chapter 9), which suggests discussions for the couples themselves.

6

Covenanting Ceremonies: Valuing the Tradition

At all weddings in Hawai'i and at two on the U.S. mainland Donald Schmidt has opened with this traditional chant:

Onaona i ka hala, me ka lehua
He hale lehua, no 'ia na ka noe
O ka'u no 'ia, e ano'i nei
E hali'a nei, ho'i o ka hiki mai
A hiki mai no 'olua, a hiki pu no me ke aloha,
Aloha e! Aloha e! Aloha e!

It is a traditional greeting used, in similar form, in a variety of settings. It provides welcome, and says in part, "This is the sight for which I have longed. Now that you have come, love has come with you. Aloha and welcome!"

Two contrasting desires pull at the clergy and couples who shape same-gender loving covenanting ceremonies. There is a strong desire to "claim" the traditional marriage liturgies of different denominations with exciting, elegant, and noncontrived adaptations. There is an equally valid desire to bring to birth new and vital liturgies so a same-gender loving ceremony does not feel like a second hand tuxedo.

Neither of these is "right" or "wrong," and some combination of both agendas probably goes into preparing the most gracious and appropriate ceremony for any particular couple. A pastor should be able to offer both a fluid adaptation of familiar words and a palette of possibilities for a unique celebration of newly achieved rights and responsibilities. Even in the context of the most conventional adapted liturgy, choosing readings—scriptural, sacred, and secular—personalizes the covenanting experience. Framing vows, whether to use or as an exercise in understanding, deepens the planning experience.

This chapter is shaped by interviews with three pastors who are gifted at shaping traditional wedding words to celebrate the marriages or covenanting ceremonies of same-gender loving couples. Donald Schmidt is currently a pastor in the state of Washington, Kathryn Schreiber, in California, and Molly Baskette, in Massachusetts.

Says Donald of his same-sex weddings, "Frankly, they have not varied much from straight weddings—largely at the request of the couple, who basically just want to 'get married.' Are they wanting to 'mimic' straight marriage? I don't think so. But I do believe they want to find themselves in the same place, and thus tend to use the same resources."

Of his own marriage, which took place in his native Canada in 2004, he remembers, "We used essentially the order of worship from the United Church of Canada worship book. Published in 2000, the book makes no assumptions of gender or orientation in the Marriage/Partnership section, and all of the vows, etc., allow for both mixed gender and same gender services."

Molly Baskette responds to a question on source materials:

> I have to admit, if I find something durable, or create it, I stick with it. I'll only add in new material if I witness a service with great, creative elements. I'm a lazy liturgist at heart. The service I use is part UCC Book of Worship, part Episcopal Book of Common Prayer (which has a most excellent sense of gravity and drama), part my own words, and likely a few other sources that I now consider my own but were really discovered somewhere else. I do love a quote

> from Gandhi, "a vow, far from closing the doorway to freedom, opens it," that I use in my prayer of invocation.

In contrast, Kathryn Schreiber changes her liturgy continually:

> My core wedding liturgy constantly shifts and grows, adapting to fit the diverse spiritual, cultural, and private interests of each person marrying. I learn each time I attend a wedding or blessed union—and make notes after worship! The amazing array of couples with whom I have worked continues to impact my understanding of marriage and the words, symbols, and rituals we use. Over the years, I've developed an evolving core liturgy, which was heavily inspired by the UCC's Book of Worship and *Interfaith Wedding Ceremonies* from Dovetail Publishing. Other favorite sources include Northstone's *The Alternative Wedding Book; The New Jewish Wedding* by Anita Diamant; *Meditations of the Heart* by Howard Thurman; *The Patterns of Our Days: Worship in the Celtic Tradition from the Iona Community*, edited by Kathy Galloway; Canticles of the Earth: Celebrating the Presence of God in Nature by F. Lynne Bachleda; and . . . any of Hafiz' poetry (translated by Daniel Landinsky)!

THIS CELEBRATION IS A GIFT OF LANGUAGE

The event itself may be named variously. Different states use different language and mean somewhat different things by the language chosen. The occasion may be called a marriage, civil union, holy union, domestic partnership, or covenant partnership. The religious community may choose to reflect the state's vocabulary but does not need to baptize it. Any commitment ceremony in a community of faith may be called a "marriage," but not every couple may wish to claim that designation. In British Columbia, Donald found that their same-sex marriage license required "husband and husband" even for a couple that used the language of "partner."

There is variety in verbs—"marry," "unite," "take as partner," "covenant," "commit," or "join in God," "in holy matrimony," or "in wedlock." There are no correct formulas or magic words. The ceremony should be intentional and consistent, reflecting a frank conversation and clear understanding between couple and officiant. In addition, happy occasions usually include early strategic communication with family members or guests who may be experiencing a same-gender loving ceremony for the first time.

Molly points out that including "Dearly Beloved" and "Marriage is not to be entered into lightly or unadvisedly, but reverently, deliberately, and in accordance with God's purposes" may seem antiquated or precious, but helps guests, particularly the hesitant or resistant, experience legitimacy. She notes, "A few little old ladies in my church, at one such formal wedding of two gay men, who before the wedding couldn't 'imagine' what it would be like, made their way through the receiving line at the end of the ceremony and gushed to me, 'That was the most *beautiful* wedding I've ever attended.'"

When dealing with traditional language: *Don't forget to change the pronouns! . . . with a writing instrument! . . . on the paper!*

THE SIGNIFICANCE OF RITUAL

It is critically important when dealing with ritual to judge what is honest and appropriate to the particular couple for this specific occasion. In other words, if the families are not unified, don't light a unity candle! Wedding ceremonies are encrusted with rituals and customs, many of them long "divorced" from their original symbolism. For the purpose of a same-gender loving ceremony some can be eliminated, some can be adapted, and some can be embraced. After all, regardless of the couple's gender, many covenanting ceremonies need Jordan almonds and the chicken dance!

The Processional

The procession is a central tradition with roots in many cultures and reflected in biblical texts. In fact, when many contemporary families gather for a rehearsal, they are not anticipating the practice of liturgical phrases so much as "walking down the aisle." This is a part of the ceremony where creative patterns in same-gender loving ceremonies already have helped redefine customs for heterosexual ceremonies. Attendants are often grouped regardless of gender beside a family member or old friend or in a circle. Nonmatching numbers of attendants are common and more diverse ages appear in the procession instead of the more traditional young adults and children. Ribbons, votive candles, or other symbols are often carried rather than the more familiar and expensive flowers. Molly suggests that a wonderful possibility is for the wedding party to bring in all the sanctuary elements—candles, flowers, and Bible, too.

She warns that the procession in a heterosexual wedding often carries theological freight that couples would reject if it were verbalized.

> Traditionally, the bride comes down the aisle on her father's arm, as a symbol of his responsibility for and caretaking of her, even if she can't stand her father, even if she's been living independently or supporting herself financially for years, even if she's in her forties. The groom, meanwhile, is waiting patiently to "receive" this responsibility. It's an odd symbol, yet one we're loath to let go. Same-sex weddings threaten, appropriately, this gendered and even misogynistic symbolism by forcing the couple to address it in a creative way.

The creative and thoughtful shaping of a processional is important because of its "standing for" the wedding in cultural expectation, the fact that it is an embodied element in a ceremony that is fairly word-dependent, and because it invites music to the celebration. Music sinks roots into the hearts and souls of couple, attendants, and guests.

Greeting, Welcome, or Invitation

The opening of the ceremony is the occasion to create from disparate friends, workmates, family, and congregation members a new community of celebration. One of the most significant issues as particular states legalize marriage and/or holy union services is an initial large group of couples who have been waiting to have pre-existing personal covenants or nonlegally binding holy unions "regularized." Many traditional wedding services imply the beginning or near beginning of an exclusive commitment of one person to another. Those words ring false for long-time couples. A simple statement addresses this:

> Today we celebrate not a fragile, fledgling commitment, but the rich unfolding of love, tenderness, and mutual support that emerge from _______ years of circumstances so often mentioned on these festive days—joy and sorrow, abundance and hard times, sickness and health.

Kathryn responds to the issue of ceremonies in which the couple come from different religious or cultural traditions and acknowledges that there are *always* guests from different traditions, and therefore . . .

> I always make it a point at all public ceremonies to invite those assembled to "make translations" throughout the ceremony, honoring their spiritual paths and convictions, trusting that there is something larger than our specific beliefs that connect us. I might say, "May our love for this couple connect us into one body for this afternoon." If I know there will be atheists or agnostics present, I make sure to say something like, "During prayer times, please hold silence or enjoy the beauty of this place if that allows you to connect with the Holy." A little bit of compassionate permission goes a long way to making everyone welcome, and one doesn't have to erase one's faith.

Molly adds this caution, "If I am the only clergy doing the wedding but am expected to represent other traditions, I do my best to learn but not to overstep or overstate my authority, or to coopt other traditions."

Pledge of Support

The three people interviewed and anecdotal evidence from clergy conversations underlines the importance of clergy who do adaptations from traditional sources using only those materials with which they are comfortable and into which the couples has had significant input. Most "contemporary traditional" services avoid the language of "giving away" in favor of a pledge of support by families, by family and friends, or by family first and then friends. In the ceremony for a same-gender loving couple the rational for using a pledge of support rather than "give / accompany" language goes deeper than the desire to completely undermine any sense in which people are property. Molly mentions that the pledge of support is the most affirmed part of her wedding services because it "undergirds this marriage with a healthy and wide-ranging base of support." She also points out that this element of liturgy forces the hesitant or resistant to face their prejudices and choose affirmation or silence. An optional children's pledge of support or couple' words of commitment to children is a significant addition but should be adapted to the ages of the children and situation. Most wedding services contain suggested language for the blessing of a new family.

Ceremony as Political Statement

Except for the pledge of support and its tacit call for witness, Molly steers clear of using same-sex weddings as political statements, even for celebrating the "breakthrough" of the possibility of marriage. Her policy is to remain in the private and personal realm. Other liturgists make different choices and Ellen Oak's liturgy for a wedding (pages 158–66) includes a civil blessing from the text of the judges' decision in *Goodridge v. Department of Health*, written by Massachusetts Supreme Court Chief Justice Margaret H. Marshall.

Kathryn takes a middle road:

> For years now, I've made mention of marriage justice in all wedding ceremonies I've performed. For heterosexual couples, I say, "Because this state allows you to marry, today's ceremony is not only social and sacred, it will also be legally binding." If there are gay and lesbian family or friends at a "straight" wedding I might take it further. I check with the couple first. When we clergy have the courage to name what is and isn't, it can be a blessing for some who've had to put themselves in a box at weddings. It can be heart-opening for those who want to expand marriage but didn't have theological permission. And it can be a poke at a hornet's nest—so be prepared! At same-gender weddings, I make sure to include mention of mixed gender couples and those who are single.

Words of Commitment, Vows, Promises

The vows, chosen or created, are the emotional center of the ceremony and many clergy, even those who do not anticipate the couple writing more of the service, encourage couples to "write their own vows," if only as an exercise. It is important that couples understand that the words of promise are identical and reciprocal. Since vows are not an appropriate opportunity to toast one another, publicly witness to fine qualities, express gratitude, or reminisce, this may be the moment to suggest a personalized "preface" to the vows. Particularly for couples together for a long time, an earlier place in the service can have a "Witness to Tenderness." Of course, reminiscences and toasts at the reception are really the "icing" on the cake.

In a Christian context, vows contain the expectation of lifelong commitment, something like "forsaking all others." This is an issue of debate and discussion as secular same-gender loving people reconsider the cultural model of monogamy. The choice for a religious service of legal marriage or faithful covenant often is made because of this distinction.

Exchange of Symbols

The ring ceremony has the same murky history as the procession. It symbolizes the transfer of land or property. While for heterosexual couples this sometimes seems the dinosaur in wedding services (again, one that few are willing to eliminate!), for same-gender loving couples, whose rights to own property together, inherit property, share insurance policies, and so on are frequently shifted by the change in legal status, the ring is a particularly potent symbol. This is also an opportunity to adapt familiar liturgy. Here's an example of liturgy expanding because these people have already been wearing these rings for years.

> The ring has long been a symbol of marriage, for, as the ring is a circle without end, it is the wish and hope of all that your marriage will endure, summer and autumn, winter and spring, through all the cycles of human life. These rings have been worn by you in wonderful days and sad ones. They are shiny with work and applause, dish soap and dinners and dog fur. Yet you take them off and put them on again today with new and special celebration.
>
> ______ , I give you this ring all over again as a symbol of my faith in you and in God's blessings and my hope for other couples who will follow us on this path. You know this and now the whole world knows—I love you.

The Kiss

Molly says this about what is often the end of the ceremony—the kiss.

> Interestingly, when I first put together the marriage ceremony I use, neither the UCC Book of Worship nor the Episcopal Book of Common Prayer included a kiss! Man, those movies and soap operas

> got it so wrong. But marrying couples like to kiss! And we like them to kiss! So I wrote it into the liturgy, "You may bind your covenant with a kiss." And same-sex couples need and deserve to kiss, just as straight couples do.

Weddings and covenanting ceremonies are filled with traditions—traditions found in books, traditions from family custom, particular ethnic traditions, even movie traditions! Individual clergy develop their own wisdom and seek from couples things that matter to them. Kathryn notes, "While I have a number of 'wedding' resources, I find that the best stuff is often not promoted as marriage or wedding content. For one wedding between two elementary school teachers, we found a children's book, Sarah S. Kilborne's *Peach and Blue*, that turned out to be one of the best texts for their wedding—expressing as it did, in story and picture, the power and grace of selfless love."

A wide range of creative original liturgical resources is offered in "Part 4: Words of Love." A true closing mirrors Donald's opening, "Now that you have come, love has come with you. Aloha and welcome!"

7

The Congregation: Fostering Healthy Conversation, Growth, and Change

Fostering effective communication, energy, and efficacy for change and healthy church growth have been emphases for pastors and congregational leaders since people first gathered in faithful communions. Clergy and lay leaders have struggled and will continue to struggle with the inevitable conflicts that arise when addressing competing needs and hopes within congregations of unique human beings. One doesn't even need issues of social change and controversy to experience this. In fact, any parish pastor will have stories about heartfelt disagreements, volatile arguments, and power struggles over everything from the location of nametags to the choice of mugs or paper cups at coffee hour.

Training clergy and empowering lay leaders to address congregational conflict and methods of resolution are important in the academic theological education for seminary students as well as in the continuing education of pastors. Denominational and multifaith resources abound. All of this is useful and good, providing help to religious leaders on a variety of topics. However, when it comes to congregational change and growth in support of and response to same-gender loving couples, there are unique factors that can make this particularly thorny and challenging, as well as invigorating and life enhancing.

Several years ago, there was a large church in a medium-sized industrial city trying to work its way through denominational resources on LGBTQ concerns. The church included a handful of visible gay and lesbian members, a combination of new and long-term members of different ages and economic levels, and a small number of people of color within a historically white community. During a small group discussion, a Latina lesbian who had recently joined the church became upset after two long-term members, both heterosexual and white, expressed their view that "the church just isn't ready for this yet." Through angry tears she said, "I joined this church because I thought you were different. You seemed so warm and welcoming—like you really wanted me here. Now, you're telling me that you don't!" In response, an older white, heterosexual man looked at her as his eyes welled up, "We *do* want you here. I do. I like you—the energy and excitement that you bring. I like that the church is getting new life. But I've been a member here for over forty years. So much is changing so fast. I feel like everyone's telling me that everything I built my life on is wrong—how I understand marriage, men and women, the Bible. It's too much too fast. It feels like someone is taking my church away from me."

This is a typical congregational experience these days—the public clashing of personal perspective, need, and experience. What is atypical is that instead of talking about each other, these people are actually talking to each other, face to face, with real emotion and vulnerability. These two individuals express truths—that the church is too slow to change for some and too fast to change for others. Both express how closely intertwined their personal sexual identity is with their place in the community of faith. Both voices are honest and valuable to the integrity of the community, as are the many other voices somewhere along the continuum of sexuality and spirituality. Both of the people in this conversation demonstrate the need for additional personal and congregational pastoral care.

There are two primary barriers that often prevent healthy conversations, growth, and change in congregations on matters of sexuality. First of all, none of us likes conflict. Most church members have not been taught how to "argue well" or "fight fairly" or even to approach conflict at all within religious settings. Even those who negotiate and manage conflict professionally often park those skills at the door of the church. In our culture we tend to assume that "conflict" means "fight" and that "fight" means winners and losers. No one wants winners and losers at church; therefore, without other more positive models of communication and negotiation, we avoid difficult and disagreeable conversations. Too often, people internalize the perception that being religious means being nice and that being nice means avoiding conflict. Thus, when disagreement and conflicts arise, as they always will when people are in relationships that matter, church members often respond in one of a few ways. Some may exchange their religious identity for their secular one in order to argue as if they are on the job. Others may abdicate their own responsibility, give up, and give in to clergy and lay leadership. Still others may withdraw their support in any number of ways or give up and go somewhere else. Obviously, none of these is truly a functional option for the individual or community.

Secondly, it is the rare congregation that helps its members understand what it means to be both sexual and spiritual human beings, much less empowers its members to create relevant, coherent, and honest personal and communal theologies of sexuality. Too often, people of faith are bombarded with media images of the marriage equality struggle and the call to take a stand as a community of faith, without a contextual understanding of the fullness of sexuality and spirituality. This is a little like being called on to referee an NCAA Final Four if you've only played in your own local league and assimilated the rules through neighborhood pick-up games. How nerve-wracking to rule on someone else's game without having studied your own—and how unfair for the players!

Historically, the church has been either the last to change or a change agent for social justice. This paradox continues to be true in the movement for queer liberation and the legal recognition to same-gender loving couples. At present, the slowness to change has created a unique set of challenges for many churches. As more states offer legal recognition of same-sex couples, and as more gay, lesbian, bisexual, and transgender couples come out, congregations are having to decide policies on marriage, union, and covenanting ceremonies in response to the requests of particular couples. Often couples will assume that if it is legal, the church will support it. After all, how many heterosexual couples wonder whether or not the church will support their decision to be married?

This creates a series of difficulties. Most people, other than deacons and pastors, have not thought about church marriage policies beyond finances and arrangements. Yet the first time a same-gender couple approaches the pastor seeking to be covenanted/married in the church, it often becomes a topic of discussion, debate, and decision-making. The couple then becomes the "test case," shifting the emphasis from their personal celebration of love and commitment to a controversy of congregational policy. Diaconates and councils experience the pressure to respond quickly, perhaps shortcutting their own discernment process. In this case, both the couple and church leadership may feel compromised, as if their own needs were somehow discounted. Church leaders don't want to hurt feelings, but they may not have the skills to avoid unnecessary pain.

In some situations, couples find that the state has legalized same-sex marriage or civil unions, but their church is unclear as to whether the pastor may officiate and whether the sanctuary should be used. Feeling inadequately prepared and overwhelmed, some congregations delay these decisions or even refuse to decide. In churches in which the leadership is in basic agreement, the members have celebrated a GLBT presence, and there is very little hidden conflict, the outcome is positive despite the awkward process. However, other congregations and couples experience deep and divisive pain at these moments, which could be managed and minimized. Developing skills in communication and conflict management may enable congregational leaders to respond in a more timely manner as well as more effectively.

In his book *A Time to Embrace: Same-Gender Relationships in Religion, Law, and Politics*, William Stacey Johnson writes:

> As a practical matter, I believe that it takes two things for religious-minded people to move from being non-affirming to affirming. The first is actual experience with gay and lesbian people who are living

> lives of integrity . . . it requires real-life experience. The second thing will be biblical and theological arguments that demonstrate the error of past moral teaching and provide persuasive reasons to begin thinking about the issue in a different way.[1]

Johnson's perspective has been proven true time and time again. In regards to ceremonies of covenant and marriage for same-gender loving couples, the topic is often avoided until necessary; and it only becomes "necessary" when a particular couple raises the issue through their personal request. Again, this can be both positive and negative. People change churches, and people change their beliefs about sexual orientation, gender identity, and marriage equality because of personal experience. Formerly held misperceptions, both conscious and unconscious, fall away when we are faced with real people whom we know, love, and respect. Relationships trump belief. Thus, the known couple that comes seeking a ceremony of marriage or union may open the door of change faster than anything else could; however, depending upon the specifics of the people in the parish, the collateral damage could be great.

The call to be faithful ministers of the gospel of justice and also supportive pastors to the individuals within our congregations is perceived by many clergy as an unavoidable conflict of interest. However, this need not be so. A traditional model of pastoral care, focused exclusively on individual counseling as separate from our communal life and the realities of social injustice, limits clergy and inhibits congregations from being fully present to the individuals, families, and communities in which we all live. Unfortunately, many of us have been trained to believe that pastoral care is what goes on behind closed doors while the work of social justice occurs in public view.

Just as the secular movement toward legalizing same-sex marriage begs religious questions of sexuality, it also calls us to develop an integrative model of pastoral care. From the beginning, feminists have claimed that the personal is political, and, indeed, this is no truer than in the care of same-gender loving couples and their families within the life of congregations. Communal pastoral care, grounded in an integrative theological core, empowers creative engagement for laity and clergy alike as we build culturally relevant and justice-oriented churches. Together, clergy and congregations must articulate what it means to be faithful communities in a multicultural and multifaith society. Pastoral theologian Joretta Marshall writes about these moments when tension arises between our ideals and realities.

> One necessary component of congregational care is to address pain that is created when the expected ideal is not matched by reality. A caregiver in a congregation listens to the voices of those who painfully feel the oppression of the institution. . . . Valuing the local community of faith does not imply a denial of ways in which communities participate in unjust or destructive practices through the reality of racism, patriarchy, or the abuse of power. The pastoral person has the task of holding up the vision of the church while, at the same time, working to eradicate the structures that diminish the church's movements toward justice.[2]

Creating change and fostering healthy growth is a byproduct of effective and theologically rooted pastoral care. Engaging congregations to reflect upon and articulate their sense of identity and purpose, while listening to the voices of those on the edge who have been hurt by church and society, and reconciling the presumed differences between justice and care, enlivens and energizes our shared ministry. Members of the same congregation who hold conflicting beliefs need the opportunity to struggle with what it means to be members of the same church with a shared common vision and theological core.

This engagement of difference does not assume that all will come to agreement, but it does require that all are offered the pastoral act of listening, valuing, and honoring their experience. Finally, we can build upon what Charles Gerkin has named a "centrifugal model of care"[3] made of permeable boundaries that expand and stretch in their reach to welcome rather than impenetrable ones that separate and narrow our focus to those within immediate view.

In summary, there are several steps that clergy, lay leaders, and congregations can take to foster healthy conversation, growth, and change in ministry with same-gender loving couples.

- Understand and articulate a model of individual and congregational pastoral care for all who are affected by same-gender loving couples that engages laity and clergy alike.
- Develop a communal vision for the church that is consistent with its identity as it seeks to engage in the questions and concerns of same-gender loving couples and families.
- Provide opportunities to learn healthy communication and conflict management skills, affirming that negotiating difference and diversity is a fact of communal life.
- Provide educational opportunities for church members to study sexuality and to develop sexual and spiritual identities, grounded in well-informed theology and psychology.
- Listen to the voices of same-gender loving couples and all GLBT persons and their family members who are willing to share their experiences of joy and pain.
- Support the development of connections and community among same-gender loving couples and their families within the congregation.
- Engage in the denominational process to become a "Welcoming/ Affirming Congregation."
- Create church policy and practice concerning marriage and covenanting ceremonies before it becomes a crisis.
- Communicate the congregation's advocacy, welcome, and support of same-gender loving couples to the surrounding community.
- Support those in the congregation who work for GLBT justice in society, and engage the congregation in the work of ending oppression and creating marriage equality.

If pastors and parishioners are willing to take this journey together, they will find themselves engaged in one of the most crucial theological endeavors of our time. Responding to the needs of same-gender loving couples, initiating communal conversation and study of sexuality and spirituality, taking our relationships with one another seriously enough to engage in difficult conversations and negotiations, reflecting upon who we understand ourselves to be as the church in our time and place, and working for justice are ingredients of the life of faith. In taking this opportunity to reflect and respond, congregations in the center may receive gifts from those at the edges and, in receiving these gifts, may find themselves moving toward that margin of social and personal oppression and liberation.

8

The Community: Public Conversations and Witness

The call of people of faith to engage in public conversation and witness to justice is neither new nor unique to the concerns of same-gender loving couples and the queer community. Wherever there has been oppression of any kind, there has been the call of liberation. God's call for justice is never silent, nor is it singular. God speaks in community, connecting us with one another into a chorus of voices speaking for those who have been hushed. Historically, people marginalized due to their sexuality are the most invisible, as if being unseen and unheard will prevent "the very stones from crying out." Yet, throughout our multicultural global family, the lives of gay, lesbian, bisexual, and transgender persons continue to shout forth their very existence, proclaiming the triumph of love. Whether gathered in upper rooms for prayer, cloistered from potential arrest, or banished into houses dependent upon others to bring food, whether surrounded by family and friends in witness of covenant, or standing vigil in government halls, the goodness of love compels lives of justice. The particulars of the struggle differ according to social and religious location, but the call to set free is one. Every time another state or country legalizes same-sex marriage, queer people living in countries and religious communities that outlaw and punish homosexuality experience healing and hope. This is the power and promise of public witness.

Even so, there is a painful paradox at work when it comes to understanding, naming, and advocating for sexual justice and liberation, which differs from the other justice concerns. Rare is the person of faith who believes that poverty, lack of health care, homelessness, or racism is acceptable in society. We may disagree as to their root causes and the appropriate response by the community of faith. However, questioning our response to social injustice or corporate evil is not the same as questioning the intrinsic moral good of a person or situation, or believing that it is a private matter, and therefore not of public concern. No worship leader hesitates to voice prayer concerns for the hungry. Yet, how many pastors hesitate before speaking public prayer for those who suffer the grief of homophobia or the rage against transgender persons? In our misperception of sexuality as a private matter, we have avoided the public conversation of heterosexist and male privilege, thereby deepening the insidious entrenchment of structures of oppression. Certainly the erotic expression of love between partners is personal and need not be on public display. However, when access to legal, financial, civil, and religious rights is based upon the gendered status and sexual expression of these partners, then the structures of domination and oppression must be named and dismantled. The language of oppression couched in religion is dangerous. Thus, the power of these overt and subtle references to religion by those who question and oppose marriage equality in the public arena cannot be ignored and unanswered. It is the congregation that has fostered healthy conversation, growth, and change grounded in its theological identity that is more equipped to move outside itself and speak the truth of justice to the power of discrimination.

As noted in the opening chapters, we are living in a time of numerous changes in our understandings and experiences of family. When the familiar structures and functions of family in society shift and move, so do the roles and relationships of individuals within the family. Sociologists, anthropologists, and family researchers point out that the institution of marriage has been rapidly shifting, long before gay marriage was on the cultural radar. As pastors and people of faith, we know that even though this process is predictable, it is challenging. All of this sea change makes us nervous, reminding us of how small we individuals really are in the big picture of human living. When we feel anxious and powerless, most of us are tempted to look for someone to blame.

How often have anxious and angry voices cried out that "gay marriage is to blame for the downfall of the institution of marriage and western civilization as we know it?" Same-gender loving couples have served as an easy target for the projections of fear and worry. It is often easier to be angry at change than to grieve the loss of what is familiar. Philosopher Rene Girard suggests that one of the means by which societies seek to achieve cohesion in times of instability is through the identification of scapegoats—individuals and categories of persons who serve as socially approved targets of rage, violence, and blame. When directed at a specific scapegoat, the chaos and confusion of social conflict is diminished, if only for a time.[1] This practice of scapegoating, familiar as well in Hebrew and Christian scripture, may lower communal anxiety in the short run, but can never lead to the acknowledgement and forgiveness of sin, the healing of reconciliation, or the empowerment of restorative justice.

In its many different manifestations, the public witness and work of justice can be both the essence and result of effective pastoral care. This is especially true in the specific work to create marriage equality and the larger struggle to end LGBTQ oppression. Too often we divide the care and nurture of congregations from the call to engage with the struggles of the world. In the lives of same-gender loving couples, the personal concerns of the relationship can rarely be separated from the realities of living within a homophobic and heterosexist society.

Joretta Marshall writes, "Genuine pastoral care is about the task of overcoming the dualism of prophet and priest as congregations embody an ecclesial vision, seeking to participate meaningfully in structures which seek justice rather than perpetuating injustice."[2] Same-gender loving couples need to know that they are not only welcome to participate in the life of a congregation, but that their lives are honored by their church.

Words of welcome without action sound hollow. Action requires us to engage with the realities of day-to-day living. Creating justice within the congregation compels us to step outside the sanctuary into the city hall, statehouse, and offices of national government, for these are the places of decision-making that affect the most personal aspects of the same-gender loving couples whose lives we bless. Providing pastoral care means that we move out of our studies into the town square, the neighborhood park, and the places of gathering if we are to change our culture's passive negligence in the face of homophobia, heterosexism, and transphobia. We must work to change the gendered social and cultural scripts that have limited our ideas about marriage and relationships; and we must interrupt the slurs that continue to be hurled at those for whom we care, rather than wait to bandage the wounds.

In his book *Discovering Images of God*, Larry Kent Graham describes prophetic action as "the individual and collective strategic effort to change the social order to be more relationally just towards all its members," and lists it as one of five dimensions of pastoral care.[3] It stands to reason that if people who have lived on the margin are going to feel valued and connected in church, then the community must stand firm in its opposition to all that is dehumanizing and oppressive. Active and visible participation is required; otherwise, care is compromised.[4] James Poling builds upon this vision of connection between care within the congregation and working for justice in society. In *Deliver Us from Evil*, he encourages people of faith to engage in "practicing goodness" and names its six dimensions as:

1. Developing a spirituality of resistance (internally identifying oneself in resisting evil rather than in oppressive structures);
2. Living in solidarity with resistance communities (acting with others in the midst of suffering);
3. Taking moral and material inventory (addressing the ways that we are privileged by the oppression of others);
4. Confronting the abuser within (owning that we have willfully overlooked or acted upon our own biases);
5. Confronting persons of power (using the power we have to confront those who abuse their power); and
6. Negotiating with institutions (shifting the emphasis from survival to justice-making in our structured and shared life).[5]

In other words, restorative justice embraces all dimensions of our congregational life, constantly pulling us outward through the centrifugal energy of caring for individuals into the public intersections of human living—the places where Jesus walked, and talked, and got into trouble.

So how do we do this? In the words of Walter Wink, how do we call the "Powers that be" away from their idolatrous deification of heterosexist and patriarchal marriage and lead them toward the fulfillment of sexual justice? How do we confront the religious platitudes, images, and appeals to scripture that saturate public discourse, serving to maintain the privileged power and elite status of those who benefit from the present structure of marriage rights and benefits? Perhaps it requires the larger and longer view, as well as the day-to-day details of change. In order to dismantle the "domination system" of violence and oppression, Wink offers four stages of engagement. First, he says that in speaking our experience, we name the Powers that dominate our lives. Second, "Unmasking the Powers takes away their invisibility, and thus their capacity to coerce us unconsciously into doing their bidding. [Third,] Engaging the powers involves joining God's endeavor to bend them back to their divine purposes." Then, fourth, in our liberation of the Powers, we redeem ourselves and the system itself from the "bondage to idolatry."[6]

NAMING AND UNMASKING THE POWERS

Naming and unmasking the powers begins at home and in community. We must start with study, reflection, and prayer if we are to discern the myriad ways in which heterosexist privilege has benefited some at the expense of others. Most members of our churches have not had the opportunity to learn about the history of marriage, and many assume that same-sex marriage is as radical as the opposition paints it. Just as the ecumenical Welcoming Church movement initiated study of sexual orientation and the reality of homophobia, the call for marriage equality can facilitate in-depth reflection on marriage and family and the impact of heterosexism. Ranging from the distribution of social security benefits to the joint ownership of property, people of faith need to know the inequities built into the present system. As we listen to same-gender loving couples who have been harmed by this system, we need to challenge heterosexual couples to address the privileged status from which they benefit. Through our learning and caring for one another, we can form a theological core moving outward to witness and work for justice. Exploring together the qualities of love and partnership not bound by gender and orientation can provide opportunity to claim what is core to our covenants and to deepen and enrich the lives of couples within congregations.

Speaking with one another about our experience rather than to one another about the issue heals and empowers more than we imagine. For example, during one study group, the heterosexual members asked a gay couple, William and Sam, to share the story of their relationship. The men talked of what had drawn them together, named some of the joys and difficulties through the years, and described the process in which they had engaged to establish some legal protection. They explained their choice not to have a public ceremony at the time of their moving in together because Sam was a teacher and nervous about backlash. In addition, they assumed that his family would not attend, since they refused to accept the relationship as anything other than "sinful." They both talked about their desire to parent and the ensuing exploration of options. In the end, they let go of the dream of raising their own children, cultivating powerful bonds with William's nieces and nephews.

Then they shared the impetus for their involvement in the movement for marriage equality, describing their pain when one of their closest friends suddenly died. They told the group that while standing in their friend's kitchen soon after his death, his parents, from who he had been estranged, arrived. Politely greeting their son's partner of decades and his long-term friends, they claimed their son's body. Specifically, they had made arrangements to have the body transported to their hometown, hundreds of miles from where he lived, for burial. On their way out of the house, they picked up some of their son's items and left.

Through the telling of this story, William and Sam realized that most of their heterosexual church friends had no idea of the realities of their lives, partly because no one had ever asked, and partly because they had kept their pain hidden. Hearing this story, the heterosexual members were shocked and angered at the level of discrimination and the depth of pain that their friends had endured. They were also deeply saddened at not having been present for William and Sam at the time of their loss, and they felt somehow complicit. Moved through tears to action, many members of the church have become actively involved in the work to legalize same-sex marriage. The congregation has taken steps to reach out into the GLBT community and more fully support those in their midst.

ENGAGING AND LIBERATING THE POWERS

The work of engagement and liberation is also the work of evangelism—proclaiming the "Good News" to the world, and inviting people to join us in communities of progressive Christianity. Far too often the label "Christian" has been collapsed into words like "conservative" and "heterosexist," especially in the arena of public witness. When clergy engage in public conversations, proclaiming congregational and denominational support for same-gender loving couples and marriage equality, the necessity of separation of church and state, and the urgency to end discrimination in legal civil marriage, many people hear a different version of the Christian faith than they have heard before. People have been moved by the hearing of this good news and have found an open door into a new spiritual home.

After testifying at legal hearings or writing letters to the local newspaper, clergy often report being approached with questions such as "Where is your church?" or "Tell me about your denomination." Those who need to hear the story of God's extravagant welcome are rarely going to step inside the church door listening for it. Rather, as we join our voices to theirs in the struggle for justice, those who "have ears, will hear."

In the spring of 2009, the New Hampshire Senate Judiciary Committee held its public hearing on HB436 calling for the legalization of same-sex marriage. Although the bill had already passed the house, and the research pointed to fairly widespread popular support, the opposition was much more visible and outspoken. Well-organized church groups and individual speakers carrying Bibles and proclaiming "the Christian view of marriage as one man and one woman" filled the hall. A few clergy and identifiable people of faith spoke in support of marriage equality and were scattered throughout the crowd.

The Rev. Gay Schulte, New Hampshire Conference Minister of the United Church of Christ, spoke in support of the bill, referencing both the work of the conference and denomination in the journey for full civil and religious equality for LGBTQ people:

> The General Synod of the United Church of Christ . . . voted to support a resolution calling for equal marriage rights for all people. . . . Working for full marriage equality is one way that we say to our LGBT brothers and sisters that they are valued and respected members of our churches and our society. . . . In advocating for the passage of this bill, I remind you that this is a matter of civil rights. Those of us in the faith community will continue to have the responsibility to decide whether or not to marry a couple. This law . . . will give the freedom to those of us who believe our faith calls us to act with justice, kindness, and care for all God's people. . . . Passage of this measure is a matter of morality, and it is the right thing to do.[7]

After hearing Rev. Schulte and other clergy speak in support of marriage equality, several persons sought them out to inquire about local congregations where same-gender loving couples, their families, and allies might be welcomed. Repeatedly, people speak their gratitude in hearing "another side" of Christianity when it comes to discussions of marriage and family.

Regardless of the response, we must speak out and visibly confront discrimination against LGBTQ persons wherever it is found. This engagement with the powers of oppression does not stop with one letter or phone call. Nor does it end with one public testimony. Rather, it calls us to a journey of engagement with all the forces and factors that prevent same-gender loving couples from living in communities of mutuality, respect, and safety; as well as the establishment of civil rights, benefits, and protections equal to those of heterosexual couples and families. Liberation of the powers that idolize heterosexual marriage and demonize same-sex marriage means that we must form inclusive and diverse communities, grounded in theologies of abundance rather than scarcity, which in turn can serve as models for others who are constricted by their own limitations regarding the gospel of love.

The Religious Declaration on Sexual Morality, Justice, and Healing, which follows, is an example of the kind of theological foundation that supports engagement of the issues of sexual injustice both within the congregation and beyond.

Religious Declaration on Sexual Morality, Justice, and Healing

Sexuality is God's life-giving and life-fulfilling gift. We come from diverse religious communities to recognize sexuality as central to our humanity and as integral to our spirituality. We are speaking out against the pain, brokenness, oppression, and loss of meaning that many experience about their sexuality.

Our faith traditions celebrate the goodness of creation, including our bodies and our sexuality. We sin when this sacred gift is abused or exploited. However, the great promise of our traditions is love, healing, and restored relationships.

Our culture needs a sexual ethic focused on personal relationships and social justice rather than particular sexual acts. All persons have the right and responsibility to lead sexual lives that express love, justice, mutuality, commitment, consent, and pleasure. Grounded in respect for the body and for the vulnerability that intimacy brings, this ethic fosters physical, emotional, and spiritual health. It accepts no double standards and applies to all persons, without regard to sex, gender, color, age, bodily condition, marital status, or sexual orientation.

God hears the cries of those who suffer from the failure of religious communities to address sexuality. We are called today to see, hear, and respond to the suffering caused by violence against women and sexual minorities, the HIV pandemic, unsustainable population growth and over-consumption, and the commercial exploitation of sexuality.

Faith communities must therefore be truth seeking, courageous, and just. We call for:

- Theological reflection that integrates the wisdom of excluded, often silenced peoples, and insights about sexuality from medicine, social science, the arts, and humanities.
- Full inclusion of women and sexual minorities in congregational life, including their ordination and the blessing of same sex unions.
- Sexuality counseling and education throughout the lifespan from trained religious leaders.

- Support for those who challenge sexual oppression and who work for justice within their congregations and denomination.

Faith communities must also advocate for sexual and spiritual wholeness in society. We call for:

- Lifelong, age appropriate sexuality education in schools, seminaries, and community settings.
- A faith-based commitment to sexual and reproductive rights, including access to voluntary contraception, abortion, and HIV/STD prevention and treatment.
- Religious leadership in movements to end sexual and social injustice.

God rejoices when we celebrate our sexuality with holiness and integrity. We, the undersigned, invite our colleagues and faith communities to join us in promoting sexual morality, justice, and healing.[8]

Imagine what might happen if our clergy and congregations took seriously the model of practicing goodness as set forth by James Poling. What might happen if we began to embody the six dimensions as they relate to the work of sexual justice and marriage equality? Obviously, we would find ourselves in some challenging moments in our personal and communal lives. Yet, we might also find the call of Micah 6:8 "to do justice and to love kindness, and to walk humbly with your God" coming alive in our midst, compelling us to take seriously the injustices of all who suffer anywhere in the system of domination. Engaging in the practice of goodness, we might find ourselves living into both the beloved community of faith, and the more perfect union of state.

Part Three

So You Want to Get Married? Unioned? Domestically Partnered?

9

Unique Conversations for Same-Gender Loving Couples

Paul the apostle, whose letters are less frequently quoted in this book than are the four Gospels, wrote some emotional, psychological, and spiritual advice to the church at Philippi, his favorite church, the one that was most generous to Paul in his times of need, the one that met in the home and through the hospitality of Lydia the merchant in purple cloth.

> Finally, beloved, whatever is true, whatever is honorable, whatever is just, whatever is pure, whatever is pleasing, whatever is commendable, if there is any excellence, and if there is anything worthy of praise, think about these things. Keep on doing the things that you have learned and received and heard and seen in me, and the God of peace will be with you. (Phil. 4:8–9)

NO AND YES!

Part 2 of this book contains two chapters from the clergy perspective on precovenanting conversations, those opportunities to reflect on interior preparation and readiness to move forward to a marriage or covenant and those opportunities to reflect specifically on the shape and substance of the ceremony with which this commitment is marked. This chapter focuses on earlier conversations every couple should have. This is private-before-public reflection about this momentous occasion and specifically the spiritual aspect of it. These conversations (plural—this depth does not happen all at once!) help a couple focus on fundamental issues. They put a brake on where to order the cake! They may be organized by a clergyperson or other officiant sending suggested conversational topics. One model is as simple as modifying and deepening the old newspaper journalist's key questions—Who? When? Why? Where? What? How?

Who? Who are we? What is our shared history and what are the growing points in each of our histories before they were shared? Can we state in a sentence or two how each of us feels about health . . . money . . . children we already have or hope to have . . . spiritual values? How do we have fun?

When? Why is this the time for a change in the commitment level of our relationship? Can we verbally express that? Is the change generated by a political change, a personal one, or both? Have either of us had earlier marriages, partnerships, significant relationships? What does that background mean for this occasion?

Why? What kind of occasion of commitment is this? Is it a legal wedding, a holy union? This is very early and these will have no future bearing—but in a forced exercise of five minutes length we will each write a "vow," as if our ceremony were scheduled for today. As we compare these two vows, what do we learn from each one and from their similarities and contrasts?

Where? What kind of sanctuary should we choose? Civil and religious spaces are both sanctuaries, particularly for same-gender loving couples. Who do we think are the witnesses and guests we'll gather? A few or many? At this early stage, who are the truly important ones? Are there special roles for them? What kind of officiant do we want and why? Are we inviting God and what does that mean?

What? How is this a party? Weddings and unions in spiritual and civil tradition and history have been about property and party. Take a few moments to consider the property, insurance, health care, and custody issues of this plan. Set these aside for a moment and think about the fun—food fun, faith fun, fiesta fun.

How? How can we do this? Let us name the sources of support that we each have—personal, relational, financial, professional, psychological, spiritual. What are resources that we share and that sustain us? If we need some particular support, where can we turn right now Where do we think we will be able to turn in the future?

What follows are two resources for precovenanting conversations that have come to us and are being passed on in original words with much gratitude because no other sources have shared them so well. The first comes from Peter Barbosa of Oakland, California, who is a former member of the UCC Coalition Council and has represented the coalition on the UCC's Hispanic Ministries Implementation Team. He is also a professor of biochemistry and immunology. He shared his thoughts in the UCC Coalition's "Covenant Conversations" resource, writing from the Latino/Latina context. Any couple using Peter's ideas to open a conversation is invited to consider and approach the personal background place of binding but also blessing—ethnic culture, family or origin, religious tradition—not with anger or apology or fear, but simply for what it is and has been in the lives of each member of a couple. A marriage or covenant is, indeed, a "landmark" time, as Peter notes in his own words.

> I think there should be a meeting or series of meetings in which the elements of culture, family, spirituality, and Christianity are discussed. It is important to take the time of preparation as spiritual counseling that aims at complete and true integration of these elements. This time in anyone's life is likely to represent a landmark, and it brings the opportunity for deep reflection and transformation. From a Latino perspective, it could serve as a time of healing from much of the cultural oppression many LGBT Christians experience. I think that many LGBT people in my culture suffer a great deal of internalized homophobia. It is not my intention to sound judgmental of my own culture, but I perceive a higher level of internal struggle among many of the gays and lesbians with whom I interact. The "landmark of marriage" is an opportunity for reflection about these issues.
>
> Some of the potential questions to reflect on, meditate on, and pray about would include, but not be limited to:

- Is your spirit in a peaceful state with your sexuality?
- Have you reached a place within your soul in which you feel whole as a LGBT person and a Christian?
- When you pray to God about marriage, what are the thoughts that come to mind?
- How do you feel you are unique as an openly gay, Latino/a Christian?
- What aspects of your Latino/a or other cultural background have served as a challenge in your journey to becoming whole and ready for marriage?
- What aspects have served as a blessing?
- How important are your Latino/a or other cultural roots in your journey with your partner?
- Does your partner understand you, your culture, and your spirituality?
- What do you think God thinks about your marriage?[1]

What do you think God thinks about your marriage? . . . There is perhaps no more profound question for a couple planning a religious ceremony of commitment. This is the kind of conversation that can continue with the scriptural, spiritual, and prayerful assistance of a clergyperson or faithful friend.

The second resource for prenuptial conversation is part of a package sent out to couples by Rev. Kathryn Schreiber, a UCC clergywoman who at the time of this writing is pastor of United Church of Hayward, UCC, in Hayward, California. In addition to a timeline of meetings, church information, and the recommendation to hire a wedding planner, Kathryn includes these questions so that the couple can ground themselves before the first pastoral visit. Most clergy would love to have couples of any orientation think about these things . . . more than, say, the color of napkins. The following section includes the essence of her premeeting correspondence.[2]

Congratulations, about-to-be-married couple!

Here are some questions for you to discuss with each other. Some couples find it easiest to work on one category at a time—so it's probably best not to plan a marathon chat and try to cover everything in one session! Just see how these questions lead you into conversation. When we next meet, I'll ask you to share with me what came up in your conversations with each other. I ask these questions because they help me learn more about your spirituality, and thus, prepare a service that will be meaningful for you both. They also provide you with an opportunity, as a couple, to learn more about each other and your expectations about religion and spirituality. Finally, these questions help all of us reflect on the deeper aspects of making commitments, especially through a holy union.

Religion and Spirituality

Religious history: Discuss with each other your previous experiences with organized religion—both what you have found meaningful and what has been problematic. Share with each other spiritual times—when you have felt connected to something larger than yourself.

Current beliefs: Consider what you now believe and talk with each other about that. Do you believe in what I call "The Big Love"—a force that is larger than humanity, even larger than our human religions, but toward which these religions point? If so, what is it like? When/where are you most likely to experience it?

Who or what has most influenced the religious/spiritual/philosophical thoughts or beliefs that you cherish?

Rituals

Human beings create rituals to mark special occasions. Weddings and blessed unions are important rituals, part of our human legacy. Rituals function on at least three levels: (a) they mark a significant passage or status change (personal), (b) they help the community relive and remember previous rituals (social), and somehow, in the mix of all that, (c) they also connect us to the immortal (divine).

Personal level: What does this wedding mean to you personally?

What does it mean to pledge yourselves to each other as a married couple?

Are there symbols or aspects of the wedding that are most important to you?

Social level: This wedding is happening within a social context. Talk a little bit about the people who are important to you as a couple.

Will they have a role to play in the official ceremony? If not, how will they mark this turning point?

Are there any considerations to keep in mind so that the wedding is meaningful to others? Are there ways you might share this event with those who won't be attending?

Are there any aspects that might be difficult or troubling to others?

Divine level: What is God (or the Life Force, or Destiny, or The Big Love) doing in and through your wedding? Where is God in all this? What is most holy to you about this event?

The Future

Becoming a family: You two are becoming a legally (if you can marry) or socially (if you cannot) recognized family by performing this public ritual. If you haven't already had children, you might choose to parent children someday. If you have or will have children, have you thought about what sort of religious upbringing you'll share with your children?

Growing as people of faith: As part of your wedding vows you are making a commitment to support each other's ongoing spiritual development. For most of us, the path of faith has its ups and downs, surprising twists and turns. That means we really can't predict where your spiritual life will lead. So I invite you to talk with each other about what expectations you have regarding religious practices and personal spiritual development and how you might support each other in this wonderfully surprising part of human life.

Love

I adore weddings because, to me, they are all about the amazing wonder and power of selfless love—a love that moves us beyond ourselves, and yet helps us be ourselves more fully. Although a private passion brought you two together, now this romance reveals the Big Love. Do either of you have any concluding thoughts to share about love with each other . . . with me?"[2]

Any of the three organizational tools—the cub reporter's summary, Peter Barbosa's nine insightful questions, or Kathryn Schreiber's serious look at faith and love—provide a wonderful beginning for a series of conversations between individuals planning to share a commitment that will change the nature of their relationship irrevocably.

And what about Paul and his letter to Lydia's house church? "Finally, beloved, whatever is true, whatever is honorable, whatever is just, whatever is pure, whatever is pleasing, whatever is commendable, if there is any excellence, and if there is anything worthy of praise, think about these things. Keep on doing the things that you have learned and received and heard and seen in me, and the God of peace will be with you" (Phil. 4:8–9).

So help the couple consider when to say, "No," and when to say, "Yes."

No: In preparing for a marriage or union ceremony it is important to root out and acknowledge some of tougher and more broken aspects of personal life. A wedding is not a combination of "whatever is bright, whatever is bubbly, whatever is jazz or cello, if there is anything floral, delicious, gorgeously dressed, and well photographed." It is much deeper than that.

Yes: But Paul's words ring true as well. This occasion is a time to honestly look at difficulties, and then choose to celebrate, focus upon, and share with others the honorable, excellent, and just, to claim the pure, to accept the commendations of others, to offer God praise. For many same-gender loving couples the new commitment is founded on a relationship that has been "learned and received" for a long time. As time passes, the balance will shift to newer relationships. In all situations, an intentional spiritual closeness in the planning process is an invitation for the God of peace to be present.

10

Relationships with Family and Friends Regarding Your Celebration

I was chatting with a pastor friend, who said to me, "These same-sex weddings are hard on widows!" "What on earth do you mean?" She went on to tell me that the overtly tender relationships of same-gender loving couples in her congregation and the beautiful weddings they shared with the whole community of faith led to regrets and recognitions among those who had not experienced such mutually nurturing relationships or whose relationships were defined more by traditional gender role distribution. "I was not loved so much; I was not cared for so gently." One woman ruefully expressed a certain level of jealousy. "Maybe it's because gays and lesbians have to fight so hard. They don't take each other for granted the way husbands and wives do."

This phenomenon is moderated by several factors. There is always an element of grass-is-greener. There are also many dysfunctional same-gender loving relationships! In fact, individuals leaving broken same-sex relationships may not receive as much consideration from work colleagues and friends just because of the stereotype of patient and loving couples waiting for a chance to be married or legally covenanted. It is hard to carry the burden of being perfect! The early same-gender divorces in Massachusetts achieved a public prominence that few straight noncelebrity divorces experience.

Another result of previewing the "landscape of wedded bliss" is that there are many same-gender loving couples who choose not to get married when it becomes legal because they are appalled by the model of heterosexual marriage. Watching various behaviors—from prenuptial suspicion to so-called "serial polygamy" and fabled, if not fully real, suburban spouse swapping—some couples prefer the nonlegal but deep emotional and spiritual commitments forged from necessity.

In spite of these reservations, my friend is correct—family and friends often admire, even envy, same-gender loving couples and are inspired by their depth of relationship and tenacity of commitment. It is certainly the case that straight engaged couples who have seen early versions of the ceremony resources in this book have asked if it would be appropriate for them to use the vows and prayers in their own weddings!

Turning to the more practical dimensions of same-gender loving couples' relationships with family and friends involves reiterating more strongly what straight couples have been learning for years. The wedding or covenanting ceremony is for the couple with a community of support that is actually supportive. Clothing, menu, guest list, and style of ceremony should always be the couple's choice, with some consideration given to specific needs of family members to be included (such as access for people with disabilities, translation for those who speak different languages, honor given to elements of religious or ethnic background without those aspects overwhelming the couple's choices). Workmates should not dictate the budget; family should not insist on a location or choose the attendants who process. It seems obvious but it is not always so clear. In the rush of planning, some couples discover that they have surrendered control that needs to be recovered!

Financial stress is a component of most contemporary weddings and unions. Sometimes the contribution of money comes with unwanted advice, particularly if the cash is attached to specific things—"we are paying for the reception . . . the clothing . . . the music . . . the flowers, so . . ." If this threatens to impact the planning experience and its inherent fun, it is appropriate for the couple to request nondesignated gifts of support.

Before leaving the topic of unwanted advice, it is important to note that some friends, family members, and work colleagues push couples toward marriage once that has become legal in a state. "Of course, you're going to make it legal!" "Do you want to have a joint wedding?" "Are you going to the courthouse or statehouse?" "Hope you will make honest women/men of each other!" Whether serious or banter—this pushing toward marriage is as much an imposition on a couple's relationship, sense of timing, and understanding of commitment as is pushing people away from marriage. Because it is motivated by love and support, it is harder to resist. However, it is crucial to the health of the relationship to do just that—resist! Kathryn Schreiber from California has a wry comment about this: "I listen pastorally to these couples, but I remind them that this is part of the shape of equality—that for ages folks have been pestering straight folks who are dating about their marriage plans!

In addition to the particular concerns, influence, and advice of family and friends, same-gender couples also face "guest list" dilemmas because close family members may not approve of their relationship or may be openly homophobic and hostile. Don't invite them! (*This, in truth, may be the best advice in this entire book—and it is faith-based advice!*) Culture is more critical than is the Christian faith of a choice to claim a "chosen family" rather than a biological one.

Many gospel texts seem to discourage biological family connections. In Matthew 10:34–39 Jesus claimed that his mission was a sword that would divide son from father, daughter from mother. In Mark 10:29–32 he promised those who had left family for his sake that they would receive new relatives in the time to come. In Luke 11:27–28 he contradicted a woman who envied his mother by saying that she was less valued than those who hear and obey God's word. In Mark 3 (paralleled in Matt. 12 and Luke 8) Jesus' family decided that he was crazy and that they should get him under control. Word was taken to him that they were waiting for him outside, but he ignored their summons, praising as a "new" family those who were surrounding him. "Who are my mother and my brothers . . . ?" he asks (Mark 3:33).

Biblical family values value the chosen family. A helpful visual image for a couple is to consider—or even draw on a piece of paper—a "family flower" instead of a "family tree." Rather than experiencing oneself as a tiny twig on a great rooted sequoia (which is how some families feel), a couple is the center of a daisy, cornflower, black-eyed susan, the center from which each petal emerges. Some petals are members of one or the other biological families, while other petals are friends from different times in life.

These metaphorical "petals" go on the invitation list. Unlike more traditional "root" systems, there is no hierarchy in the invitations. A loving nephew may be invited, but his parent, who is the sibling of one of the partners, can be avoided. Individuals do not have their connection through someone else. There is also no need for numeric parity or degree of "relativity" balance between the two families involved. Most weddings no longer physically divide people into pews or "sides" of family and friends of each partner. People who are invited are "friends of the couple," and ushers can remind guests of this.

In the resources section there is a "Prayer of exclusion, inclusion, and forgiveness" (page 168) that may be helpful as couples consider those "we choose not to invite to the celebration of our wedding/union because their opinions damage the sacredness of this occasion" and those "we are including even though they may not accept the invitation to our wedding/union. We are saddened by their hesitation in love but wish to offer them this responsibility. We will rejoice in their presence, respect their absence, and trust their courtesy." Accepting a wedding invitation may be an act of courage and an opportunity for conversion for someone who has not had occasion to consider the issues. The couple should be certain that "borderline" invitees are safe and are not primed to generate controversy that destroys the happiness of everyone else. There may be necessary regret that not inviting some toxic individual causes the unwished-for absence of his or her spouse or young child.

Change happens, even with the most difficult of family members. Sometimes the marriage itself, the wearing down of time, or shared experiences of caring for elders lead to a future reconciliation, which might seem as miraculous as wine in a water jar.

Forgiving people cruel words and actions of the past—not saying that what they have said and done was acceptable, but that its power for hurt and harm is finished—may be an important part of the prewedding planning. Nevertheless, once a couple has decided whom to invite, it is important to let those decisions stand. Second-guessing is a first-class nuisance. One partner's family may be more fully represented than the other. There may be more friends than family. There may be more children than adults. Ex-spouses and ex-inlaws may be surprising but appropriate members of the "family." Happiness does not come from a guest list. Unhappiness sometimes does!

The most serious issue is the inclusion of children from previous marriages and partnerships. This is true in any second or third relationship and the effort and compromise involved in having their willing presence is worthwhile. Every situation is different and should be handled with integrity and gentleness. Some young people want to be attendants or to be included with a verbal commitment. Others do not want that kind of attention or to have their ambivalence "outed." While some of the ceremonies included in our resources offer language for parent/child covenant, a later opportunity for a more private family blessing occasion is equally meaningful.

At any ceremony during the next twenty years some people will be attending their first experience of a same-gender loving ceremony. These folks may feel awkward and they will feel awkward that they are feeling awkward! Helping them to relax is an important part of hospitality. A sample "Words of Welcome" to be said or printed in a bulletin is included in the resources (pages 166–67). Acknowledging the fact that people may be new to a ceremony with two men or two women will bring down the level of anxiety. Of course, there are very few differences, but guests may not know this. Many people assume that an early legal ceremony will have some political dimension. There may be a petition to sign! Worse than that—they are afraid that they will say something wrong! Some simple breaking the ice is a welcome gesture.

Another recommendation, which has been mentioned earlier, is the importance of a rehearsal for any same-sex wedding or union, however casual. This can even be scheduled earlier in the day of the ceremony. Celebrations that invite many—a whole congregation—to the ceremony, with a more select reception to follow, help broaden social familiarity with same-gender loving marriage. Willingness to extend this hospitality is a gift to future couples. A second effect is to demonstrate to still hesitant family members how accepted a couple is in a community of faith.

A final helpful suggestion is the assignment of some independent person—perhaps the clergyperson, officiant, wedding planner, or a trusted friend with no other responsibility—to handle "guest issues" on the day of the ceremony. The couple should not need to deal with someone who has decided not to come or is late or is crashing or is overserved. Even a person who is the everything and everyone "fixer" for all the other days of his or her life needs to let go of this responsibility on this special day of commitment. This is a day to look into one another's eyes and feel a circle of support so strong that memories of the past, fears for the future, and even the worry that one will trip over one's own feet dancing are buoyed up by a community of love.

11

Why Are You Inviting God?

This is not a book of theology. This book does not set out to prove to those who are doubtful or hostile that same-sex marriage is blessed in the eyes of God. There are many books with that significant agenda. Same-sex marriage blessed by God? Same-sex marriage blessed by God liturgically? Well, of course. That's the perspective of this book. And then again, maybe not . . . maybe not! There are some reasons and some situations in which couples choose not to invite God into a wedding ceremony. We will consider those before we continue.

Many human religious practitioners have and continue to bludgeon and belittle, demean, denounce, and damn same-gender loving couples in the name of God. It is easy to reject religious language altogether as somehow tainted by these curses. There will probably be people invited to any wedding ceremony who have felt so damaged by experiences in their own religious background that the very mention of God is painful to them. Others may applaud traditional Christian language, but from a motivation of revenge. "You're really sticking it to them, aren't you?!" That may be momentarily satisfying, but it is spiritually damaging. Another situation occurs when some family members from particular religious backgrounds will want to be supportive "in some sense" of the new legal relationship but consider invoking religious language a "travesty." In the time of Jesus himself, all weddings were secular occasions. Some Christians, because of their own background or sensitive to the scars of friends and reservations of relations, choose to have a private moment of prayer before the ceremony or to have a clergyperson bless the rings in advance but then proceed with a meaningful and grace-ful but fully secular public wedding. God blesses those marriages whether the word "God" is spoken aloud or not.

Let us repeat: You are not a bad person or a bad Christian if you choose to have a civil ceremony—like the wedding at Cana at which Jesus made such a contribution to the party. You are not a bad couple if one person uses more religious language than the other person in the ceremony. That happens frequently in weddings and most guests never notice. You are not bad Christians if the language you use for your ceremony opens up to include spiritualities rooted in a wide variety of traditions.

In fact, God has already been invited into your life and your relationship whether or not liturgy that invokes God is included in a ceremony, and whether or not a couple chooses to have a ceremony! Committed same-gender loving relationships are blessed and sustained and enfolded and enlivened by God. Scripture claims that God is love and everyone who loves is born of God and knows God (1 John 4:7). There is an insidious trap that goes something like this, "If you legally can get married, you should get married." This is not true. In fact, once laws change, every couple needs to consider the implications of the external situation on their particular relationship. The same holds true for religious marriage. As the heritage wedding liturgy says, marriage is to be entered into "reverently and not lightly." God loves those who do and those who do not walk down an aisle.

Most people, however, who have read this far in this book have decided to use specifically religious, faith-based language in their wedding and to prayerfully invite God into their married lives. As long as sacred terminology is not thrown into a ritual with an "in your face" flippancy or because "someone else" wants it or because weddings in movies have it, claiming religious language for same-gender loving weddings, modeling faithful covenant liturgy, and celebrating the hospitality of sanctuaries is a wonderful choice. The liturgy is a wedding gift from the couple to the world and specifically to those who will be married in years to come. The use of a sanctuary, when that is appropriate and possible, is also a source of pride to church members, encouragement to those with whom they share the experience (a niece in Kalamazoo, that old school friend in Sarasota), and a source of challenge and joy to those who are also welcomed into the building itself for reasons other than worship—from AA members to daycare parents. In fact, the very newspaper announcement of a wedding in First Saint Main Street Church may occasion a crack in somebody's closet door or somebody else's stiff self-righteousness. Bless you! The event of the wedding, your wedding, is important to you, but it is also—now and for many years to come, here and in ripples far away—"holy groundbreaking."

Faith-based language is something you can claim because there are denominations that support you and stand behind you and are not even tempted to apologize for your love! There will be more (God willing) by the time this book is published, but there are at least the United Church of Christ, the Unitarian Universalist Church, the Episcopal Church in America, the Evangelical Lutheran Church in America, and the Metropolitan Community Church. Faith-based language is also something you can claim because there are clergy in a wide range of denominations who support your wedding because God has spoken in their hearts.

GOD'S BLESSING

God enjoys a wedding, as is clear from that first miracle of Jesus, the "vintage" miracle. Faith-based language in the ceremony invites God to take part not only in the wedding but in the marriage that follows. And marriages need lots of miracles, at least several barrels-full a year! (John 2:1–10).

God understands that same-gender loving couples have been waiting for a long time for legal marriages. Waiting for a wedding is lifted up in Jesus' parable told in Matthew about the wedding attendants, half of whom brought extra oil for the long wait and half of whom let their lamps burn out. That, too, is a good story for a contemporary wedding as state after state legalizes marriage, and even as gains are temporarily reversed, because it applauds those who hold on to extra energy, effort, patience, and love (Matt. 25:1–13).

God blesses those who have come late to legal marriage equally with those who have been marrying for a long, long time. Jesus tells a parable about workers in a vineyard—some were hired in the morning, but the owner kept including others at nine, noon, three, and five o'clock. When wages were dispensed at the end of the day, the early grape-pickers were outraged that the one-hour employees received the same pay. The owner wondered why they begrudged a simple act of generosity. In parallel to this parable (Matt. 20: 1-16), God must be startled at the stinginess of heterosexual couples who have had so many years to create their beautiful or deplorable marriages and are unwilling to share this challenging gift with others!

In Ecclesiastes the value of a couple is affirmed—two together have a good reward for their toil and they have the ability to lift one another up when one falls. When a couple lie together they keep each other warm, and while a single one can be defeated, two will withstand much strain. After saying all these things about the value of two, a couple, then comes this line: "A threefold cord is not quickly broken" (Eccles. 4:12). God provides a "third strand."

Getting married is hard work but being married is harder work. Even for people who have been together for a long time marriage is something new. Biblical resources and religious language are supports to marriage. What the Bible does not do, contrary to bumper stickers, is present marriage as one woman and one man—there are as many biblical shapes of marriages and kinds of relationships as human beings can imagine. When there is integrity in relationships, the scripture affirms and supports them. When there is abuse, and there are many biblical examples of that human phenomenon, no relationships are blessed. What the Bible does do is present the ideal of marriage, the possibility of marriage, the grace of marriage as a blessed permanent situation. What—those whom—God has joined, let no one put asunder (Matt. 19:6; Mark 10:9).

EXPECTATIONS IN A FAITH-BASED CEREMONY

There are expectations in the wedding or covenant service itself—the ingredients of it—when God is invited. The liturgical (God-words) and spiritual (God-presence) aspects of marriage include some optional aspects: reading of scriptures that remind people of the stories of faith, occasionally the singing of sacred music, the well-wishing homily of clergy. These are graceful and grace-filled elements in a ceremony. There are, however, three integral functions in every religious ceremony—witness, prayer, and blessing.

In a faith-based ceremony, the promises and pledges of family and friends and the vows of the couple are made with God as a witness in addition to the witness of those who have come to celebrate and party. Some people think that's just an infidelity-preventative. No one's going to cheat on a God-witnessed vow, right? If God had eyes to roll, God would be rolling them! Better to think of such a vow as God's sustaining companionship when only one of you is holding on to the promise.

Here is the story: someday a partner, a man or a woman who is so full of wit and joy and affection on a wonderful wedding day, will sit among the mental debris of Alzheimer's disease or some other form of loss—terrible or gentle. And God will firmly hold that side of the vow so that the other partner has the courage not to step off the cliff of loneliness. Marriage vows in the name of God don't make God a supernatural private detective, but assure you that nothing that happens, even Paul the Apostle's expert list of life-challenges—hardship, distress, persecution, famine, nakedness, peril, sword, things to come, things present, powers, height, depth, angels, rulers . . . (Rom. 8:31–39)—can separate you from the love of God in Christ Jesus that holds God-committed human relationships together.

In a faith-based ceremony there are also prayers. There are prayers of thanksgiving that acknowledge the wonder of a couple finding one another, delighting in one another, and sticking with one another. There are prayers of celebration for the wedding itself—the faith and the food and the fun. There are prayers for courage, patience, honesty, tenderness, discernment, understanding—all those hope-prescriptions that may need to be filled for future diagnoses. There are prayers for family members and friends who are present, that God will bless their relationships even as they are encouraged and inspired by this celebration. There are also prayers for family and friends who are not present, that barriers will open and relationships will heal.

Prayer is not a ritual flourish for a pretty pageant, but a real "server" for ongoing communication. The prayers in the wedding remind everyone that prayer is a resource for the marriage and for all of life.

In a faith-based ceremony, there are blessings. The most common traditional form involves the officiant placing a hand on each person's head. Another involves binding the couple's hands together. (See page 140 for a service of handfasting) Still others are made visible and tangible by the lifting up of rings or the lighting of one candle from two. There are many other blessings—with seeds or honey or water. At the end of a ceremony there is a blessing on everyone present—believers, questioners, unbelievers, and the waiter who wanders through—an indiscriminate blessing that taps into the intense love of the couple—you—and spreads some of that mystery on everyone. These words-with-incarnate-expression sometimes offer specific holy well-wishes, a general sacredness upon which to draw in the "worse," "poor," and "sickness" side of the equation, and an embodied experience that reminds the couple that marriage is very much about the wonderful and yet newly limited joy of the body. The blessing has the pleasure of particularity that comes with the responsibility of exclusivity. Monogamy is blessed! It isn't for everyone—and it shouldn't be for everyone. But everyone should have the right to such a red-hot, sexy laying on of hands.

There are those who want to invite God to their wedding who haven't read any of the scriptures that have been cited. They may not have had a traditional upbringing. Luck and grace have kept them from experiencing the corrosive criticisms of some faith communities. And yet, they know they want a Higher Power, the Divine, the One whom Kathryn Schreiber calls the "Big Love" at their head table, because they have heard that this One invites the last and the least likely to a wedding banquet that has no end. For those who find scripture a little bit foreign for themselves or their wedding guests, here is one more image of invitation and affirmation.

I used to sing to my two children when they were young enough not to flee my bad pitch:

> Hush, little baby, don't say a word, Mama's going to buy you
> a mockingbird.

If that mockingbird don't sing, Mama's going to buy you a
diamond ring.
If that diamond ring turns brass, Mama's going to buy you a
looking glass.
If that looking glass gets broke, Mama's going to buy you a
billy-goat.

This traditional lullaby stopped their crying and gentled them down to sleep. Of course, I worried that I was teaching them to be infant consumers with all that "buying." Actually, what they heard, I now believe, was that the "Parent," the one who was caring for them, would take every circumstance, no matter how disappointing or frightening or sad, and improvise to bring them joy. It is, in fact, the other side of the comfort from Margaret Wise Brown's classic story, *The Runaway Bunny*, in which the child finds ways to escape, always with the hope that the Parent will turn into fisher, mountain climber, gardener, tree, wind, tightrope walker—whatever is needed.

You are inviting the great Shape-Changer God, the Trinity-Infinity, the Holy One, to your wedding and your marriage. It is worthwhile claiming one last scripture text from the very end of the Bible, from Revelation, that most culturally opaque of books. This verse does not belong, however, to those who want to interpret God as God has never been—one who is willing to leave beloved children behind. The Bible ends with a brilliantly lucid and fiercely tender image that God's reversal of all death and suffering and tears is most like . . . a wedding (Rev. 21:1–5)!

Part Four

Words of Love

12

Resources for Ceremonies

We celebrate the appropriate and blessed use of traditional wedding liturgy for same-gender loving marriage ceremonies, but we also remember that Jesus said to his disciples, "No one puts new wine into old wineskins; otherwise the new wine will burst the skins and will be spilled, and the skins will be destroyed. But new wine must be put into fresh wineskins" (Luke 5:37–38). There is a great need for fresh words and creative liturgy. A diverse group of contributors from the United States and England have responded to a request for original resources. The youngest contributor is in his twenties; the oldest is eighty-nine! All of these people are thrilled to think that their words will be shared. Permission is freely given for use of these resources in wedding, covenanting, and union ceremonies. For other uses please contact The Pilgrim Press and you will be directed to the proper source.

And, yes!! We are guessing that a great many heterosexual couples will be borrowing this material as well. That guessing is a blessing!

There are five sections of material we have collected and we recommend a review of the breadth of it. Feel free to combine these words in different ways, combine some of them with your own words, or use these words as a stimulus to your own creativity. There are "Gathering Words, Poems, and Special Prayers," "Vows and Pledges of Support," "Blessings, Rituals, and the Sacrament of Holy Communion," "Complete Ceremonies" (one sample each of four very different styles are offered), and "Birdseed and Petals—Some Scattered Words" (this has a number of prayers or statements for very specific occasions).

Enjoy! Rejoice! Play! Pray!

GATHERING WORDS, POEMS, AND SPECIAL PRAYERS

Call to Love

The One who is the source of all things
and from whom all life flows
has called you forth this day in the presence of family and friends
that your commitment to one another
may reflect the eternal love of God back into the world
where all who will affirm it may partake in its gifts.

Amen and Blessed Be.

Craig M. Nowak

Under a Strawberry Moon

One day I see you
in an apple tree, a vast, pale blossom
freed and floating up . . .

—Jean Pedrick, "Flower Moon"

Deciding to be married
is an act of imagination
like seeing the moon
as a pale blossom
or a buoy anchored near Orion
marking a space channel
or a huge burnished coin

dropping through a cloud slot
into evening.

Having imagined, now
you can time your lives together
by frosts and harvests and blooming
a month at a time
beginning tonight
under a strawberry moon.

Marie Harris

A Morning Prayer on the Day of the Service

I am nervous, O God . . . nervous that I am not good enough, nervous that I won't be able to keep my promises, much less dress right, speak right, and act right. I am not as much as I want to be for ______ . Maybe I never will be. But ______ loves me anyway, you love me anyway, and I am awake on this day of transformation. Thank you. Thank you. Thank you. And let my nervousness disappear. Let something like calm take its place. Let me get out of my own way and forget about myself in time to be happy, today, and all the days to come. Amen.

Donna Schaper

Words of Welcome

We gather today to encircle ______ and ______ with our love, to bear witness and bless the vows uniting them in the marriage of heart, body, and soul. We also gather to celebrate the reality that as humans, created in the image of God, we have been given the gift of tender hearts—open to possibilities of love and given the freedom to enter into covenants of mutuality and care. A covenant relationship is meant to be the full expression of love between two people: a sign to all they meet that they belong to each other with affection and tenderness. It is a commitment entered into prayerfully, thoughtfully, and with reverence for the great gift that it is. To this moment, _____ and _____ each bring a heart full of cherished moments as well as their hopes and dreams for the future life together. They also bring unique and complementary gifts, which flow together to form the beauty of their relationship. In a world where love may be offered without commitment, and commitments made without love, we give thanks to God for this sacred bond and holy union full of grace.

Laura Rose

Welcome to a Marriage

Welcome, all of you, to this special and joyous celebration of marriage. Born in the antiquity of our tribes and clans, nursed in the needs of our bodies and souls for sharing, nurtured in the desire to commit oneself to another person—marriage is a unique state of being together, through the bad times and the good times, the mountains and the valleys, the separations and the coming together. Let us all rejoice and be glad for the celebration of this special time.

There are many pleasures in this life, but no human possibility surpasses, I think, the wonder of being close to another human being—of sharing your life, of saying to another: you matter to me. I see you and hear you and I respond to you. That is a spiritual and physical happening of great import.

This is the celebration of commitment in the midst of your freedoms, a time of bonding, human in its fragility, divine in its aspiration, a place where you become responsible in loving care and loyalty to another person. Taste this precious moment in all its bittersweet quality and savor it often in your years together. Remember today that a wedding is not a celebration of two people becoming one. Each of you is too much your own person to accept that. Indeed, the wedding celebrates both of you continuing to become more fully yourselves, nurtured by your differences, strengthened by your opposites, growing in your diversities. The cement that binds this relationship is a miracle called love.[1]

Howard Moody

Architects of Love

You are the architects of love.
You are the contractors of happiness.
You are the builders of home.

You make your plans from story and from dream,
And trace them out on random bits of cloth.
Poets of the forest stream,
Artists of the city scene,
You sketch a life to occupy them both.

Your house is ample with room enough for two,
And visitors arriving from your past.
Building possibility,
Architects of love, you see
Ever after through each pane of glass.

What's love but a construct of memory
Fashioned with the tools you find?
What's love but a construct of memory
Colored by desire's design?

Marie Harris

Invitation to Gathering

In the midst of a world
where too many people are burdened by indifference
and too many places shattered by violence,
we gather to rejoice in the power of love!

We bear witness to love:
that of God, source of hope,
that of ______ and ______ , cause for celebration,
that of community, channel of strength,
that of enemies, gateway to peace.

God, Creator; Christ, Redeemer; and Spirit, Sustainer,
as we worship you,
fill this congregation, the couple in our midst,
and the world around us
with love overflowing and transforming!

Ann B. Day

A Prayer to Open the Service

Holy God, Blessed Spirit, you whom some call Yahweh, and others Allah, you whom some call Jesus and others Christ, you whom some know as breath or force or *ruach* or Adonai, you beyond any human name or cage, you who transcend the cages we place you in, draw near now and bless this time and place. Let the vows that are spoken be real, let the people who hear them renew the promises they too have made. Hold the space for us as a cosmic canopy and let us shiver with the grace of your presence. Open the doors on all the cages everywhere and let your people breathe free, just as you intended. Let the partnership that emerges at the end of this time renew and be new; let the feast that follows be such a sign of your kind of time that we are newly hungry for an end to any kind of smallness and any kind of poverty. And bless the two who make promises. Let them be as light as lace and as strong as wrought iron.

Thank you for letting us be here, now. Amen.

Donna Schaper

Opening Prayer

God of Isaac and Rebekah, of Naomi and Ruth, of Jonathan and David, of Mary and Joseph, of Paul and Timothy—through every generation you have inspired us to love, to leave behind isolation and independence for community and companionship. You show us the path of love and guide us continually on it. Be with us today, as we acknowledge the love of ______ and ______ , that each of us gathered here might lend to this occasion our blessings and support. In the name of all that is good on this earth, we say: Amen.

Greg Morisse

Aubade: Wedding Morning

Mountain and morning drenched in the mist,
Shadows the dawn will softly kiss,
Still the hour, fresh is the day
Into whose light you're walking.

Pack your histories, balance them well,
They are the stories you will tell.
Keep this hour, carry this dawn
Into the lives you're joining.

Greet the morning bursting with light,
Promise each other dreams of flight.
Full the hour, ageless the hope
Into the world you're borning.

Marie Harris

Gathering for a Ceremony

We'll begin with these words by William Shakespeare, from *As You Like It:*

No sooner met but they looked;
No sooner looked but they loved;
No sooner loved but they sighed;
No sooner sighed but they asked one another the reason;
No sooner knew the reason but they sought the remedy.

Family and friends, we are gathered here to celebrate the life abundant—the look, the love, the sigh, the reason and remedy. We are to celebrate the marriage of _____ and _____ . Theirs is a relationship built in love, tempered by trust, given shape in their togetherness. In love, they know joy, and in love they know what it is to share themselves completely with one another. Today their joy is multiplied as their lives become a blessing for others. Let us enter into this celebration, confident that as love is present, life abounds! We pause for a moment to open our hearts to the presence of all that is Holy.

Prayer

Holiness . . .
in the shifting of the wind,
in the sun as it plays upon the grass,
in colors—green, yellow, and blue
in two people having come to give themselves to one another.

All this is Holy. This day like the first day, this day is the first day.
Holy, Holy, Holy. All this is blessed. May it always be so. Amen.

David Parks-Ramage

Welcome and Gathering Words

Dearly beloved, out of care and affection for _____ and _____ , we are gathered here in the sight of God to witness and bless their mutual vows. To this moment they bring the fullness of their hearts and all the love and care that they have shared with one another. They bring the hopes and dreams that inspire their lives. They bring two unique personalities and spirits out of which grows the unique reality of their relationship. The words and rituals we participate in today are not magic, but a beautiful public testimony to the inner truth of their commitment. As their community of support, each of us is given the honor to share the blessing and joy of this holy union and to pledge our support of this relationship based on loyalty, trust, respect, and love.

Let us pray . . .

Loving Creator, maker of the stars and weaver of the human heart, we acknowledge your presence with us as the unifying power that has brought ______ and ______ here to declare their love and commitment to one another in this public ceremony. Love flows freely from you, uniting us in one human family.

We rejoice that these beloved ones have invited us to witness their covenant vows and we pray that they sense the support and love that we pour out toward them this day. We pray that your Spirit sustain them, day by day, as they journey through the rest of their lives together and that they may know a deep peace, grounding and sustaining them whatever the ebbs and flows of life may bring. May they return to laughter, like a wave of refreshment, as they seek each day to live out the commitment they have made to one another. Give each of them the strength and the patience to love each other well and to practice living generously with one another and all those who cross their paths. Grant to them a love that will sustain them in times of hardship and that will deepen over time and broaden through shared experiences.

As we celebrate the blessing of ______ and ______ 's love for one another, may we also be mindful of the ways you touch our lives with a variety of loving relationships. We give thanks for the ability to give and receive love and for all the people who make your love real in our lives. We pray that in some small way our time together in this place will deepen our own ability to be loving and compassionate people. We offer this prayer, bound together by the Spirit of God who dwells in us and among us: an everlasting spring that waters our souls, softens our hearts, and dances for joy whenever and wherever two people declare their love and commitment to one another. Amen.

Laura Rose

Invitation to Gathering (based on Psalm 100)

Gathered in peace on this *(spring/summer, etc.) (afternoon/evening, etc.)*,
let us make a joyful noise to God!
With singing stars and whispering winds,
we worship God with gladness!

May we know once more, in our heart of hearts,
that God has made us; we belong to the Holy One.
We are God's people, one and all.
So let us come with thanksgiving and bless God's name!
For God is good,
showering creation with steadfast love
and faithfulness which endures to all generations.

Ann B. Day

Biplane

So here you are in goggles and white silk scarves. You have reached the point of no return, the square of sky labeled DO NOT TURN BACK.
NOT ENOUGH FUEL. There's nowhere to go but into the clouds, streaked and purpled with sunset. You look at each other but cannot speak above the din of wind and propeller. You smile bravely, two movie stars in an impossible plot. Night comes. The wings begin to ice up. The engine misses a beat. The instruments are on the fritz.
We know the story . . . with a few variations, it's an old one, but it still has power to make us hold our breath or clutch someone's hand in the dark. (Will they make it? Can they hold out until dawn? Will the cloud cover tear for an instant, revealing a plowed field, a deserted beach, some rough landing place?)

You are the heroes we want to believe in. May you keep us in suspense forever.[2]

Marie Harris

Opening Prayer and Passing of the Peace

O God of David, who fought giants and loved Jonathan and wrote psalms, God of his grandmother Ruth and his many times grandchild Jesus, we come on this day with cups overflowing. We come this day with grateful songs to be sung. We come to this sacred space in expectation that here we might remember our eternal truth. We remember this afternoon all those beloved saints who have walked with us, but who are not here. We lift up their memory and invoke their love to bless this special time.

Spirit of Love, you who come into this world by many names and in many ways, we ask that you sanctify this day for us. We ask that you bless this ritual for ______ and ______ . Flow through the air that we might breathe your blessed peace. Light this sanctuary with your fire that we might better see the faces of our friends and family and know that we are home. Amen.

The followers and friends of Jesus were a motley crew: fishers and tax collectors, young and old, men and women, faithful and wavering, hopeful and afraid. On Easter morning, when he appeared to them, locked in their despair, Jesus reassured them by saying: "Peace be with you." This tremendous gift—the eternal and foundational assurance that we are well with one another and with the divine—was not given to these few so that they might keep it. Rather, this gift is meant to be given away.

Each of you came to this place by a different road. For some that long journey involved packing bags and boarding planes, long car rides and the like. For some the journey was an inward struggle to discover your strength and realize your tremendous worth—to God and to us.

Regardless of journeys past or destinations future, right now we pause to acknowledge one another and bear witness to each person's presence. The ceremony of marriage does not just mark something new, but recognizes that which has already come together. And you, all of you, are part of this. Without each of you, and many others, we would not be here today. So I invite you now, briefly, to extend this gift of peace to those around you. "Peace be with you."

Greg Morisse

Gathering Words (from Ecclesiastes 4)

Two are better than one, for if they fall, one will lift up the other. If two people lie together they generate heat to keep one another warm.

Two lives bound together can withstand more than one can alone. When the cords of two separate lives are woven together, strength is multiplied. Joy is multiplied. Common values are multiplied. Wonder and appreciation are multiplied. Generosity and hospitality are multiplied. Love for family and neighbor is multiplied. What an incredible gift it is when what has been scattered and separate, what has formerly been split right down the middle, suddenly is gathered together.

Laura Rose

Approaches

If you work alone
you will accomplish certain things:

shelled peas (do this on a porch; use an old pan)
dug post holes (pretend that China is just below each bite of the shovel)
hung laundry (click of rope through the pulley, snap of wet cotton)
picked blueberries (oh, the fragrant repetitions!)
furled sails

If you work together
you will accomplish the same things
differently, with space
for a lifetime
of conversation.

Marie Harris

Words of Gathering

Dearly Beloved, welcome to this place and this time. We gather to celebrate the love and the family that ______ and ______ have created and to bless their future as love grows.

Gracious and Holy One, with joy we turn to you today, for love is your creation and it is very good. Thank you for what has been, thank you for what is now, and thank you for what will be. May your blessing be felt and your guidance known in the words we say and the hopes we bring. Thank you for the movement of your Spirit here today. Amen.

Now, I invite the blessing of all present. Take a moment and let your affection for ______ and ______ well up within you. Notice what hopes you hold for them. Now, from the fullness of your hearts, please repeat after me, "We bless you, ______ and ______. We hope good things for you."

______ and ______, we do hope good things for you, both singly and together. Marriage is the adventure of a lifetime. It is a noble undertaking. You know it is not always easy, but there is nothing you would rather do than continue on this adventure and build an ever-changing, soul-satisfying relationship.

One gift you can bring to this growing and evolving love is an old-fashioned word: faithfulness. I charge you to have faith in your dreams of unity and harmony. Have faith in the deep feelings that brought you here today, which we honor and celebrate. Have faith that a good marriage is possible in the world we live in today. Have faith and work through whatever life brings and do it together. Trust the expansiveness of love lived out daily. Have faith—believe in yourselves; you have unique and special gifts to give each other and the world. Believe also in the God of love and mercy, who is the source of respect, hope, and renewal.

Nancy M. McKay

A Prayer of Blessing on the First Morning as a Married Couple

Before the pictures arrive or the party is cleaned up, before the first cup of coffee or the first regret, let me kiss you and hold you as though I know who you are. Let me be present to you. Keep me from running by the great moments of my life as though they didn't really happen or I wasn't really there. Slow me down and let me walk, again and again, down the aisle, up to the cake, over to someone I don't know. Let me be surprised by what really happened as opposed to what I thought would happen. Let me relish and repeat, rejoice and evaluate, open the many gifts slowly as though each were the only one. Let me light a candle on this first anniversary and each one to come. Let me be a person who collects joy. Amen.

Donna Schaper

River, Bed

Like the freshet
that wells from some
deep and secret place,
rises and spills
over scree, eddies around
ankles of fern, swells
into a leaf-carrying
stone-carrying
earth-carving stream,
stronger and stronger,
full and purposeful
as it yearns
toward the river,
the inevitable sea . . .
like that
love will describe
its long
deepening course
through the terrain
of our lives.

Marie Harris

Litany of Invocation (Isaiah 55)

Come to the waters, you who are thirsty.
You who are hungry, come to the feast.

Sweet Spirit, you have many names and call us with many voices. We come to you now, from many traditions; we respond to your presence in our own ways. May the variety of our lives, and the diversity of our beliefs, create a harmony worth singing. May the common threads of our experience, and the shared journey that we walk, create a story worth telling.

Stand in the presence of healing water, you who are sick.
You who know despair, discover the horizon line of possibility.

Spirit of life and death, fill this space with your power and strength. In these moments as we gather, to mourn and celebrate, to remember and retell: bind our wounds, fill the empty spaces inside, inspire us to sing glad songs for a better tomorrow.

All you who labor, find your rest here beside the holy.
You who are idle and aimless, hear a call to action.

Spirit of justice and compassion, speak to us again through the voice of our ancestors and all those who have gone before us. Reassure us that our work has meaning, that our struggle has purpose. Ignite in us a passion to grow the seeds of goodness and peace. Show us what wonders our love can accomplish.

You who have been blessed, be a blessing for those around you.
You who have something to be grateful for, give thanks.

Powerful Spirit, you are the joy that sparks laughter and the love that brings tears. Take this humble space and make it more than it is. As we gather to consecrate these two people in the bond of marriage, bless us with assurance and grace. As we gather to revel in the power of love to overcome life's burdens, bless us with hope and perseverance. As we gather to live out your command to love each other, bless us with courage and confidence.

Come to the waters, you who are thirsty.
You who are hungry, come to the feast.

Greg Morisse

VOWS AND PLEDGES OF SUPPORT

To you I give my heart, I give my soul, I give my very self;
Into your hands I place my hopes and dreams, my strength
and weakness.
To you I give my trust, my highest and my best.
To you and only you will I be forever true.[3]

Jonathan Blake

NAME 1: You are my home. No matter where we are, you give me a hug, and I am home. I promise to be home for you.

NAME 2: You are the source of my fun and my laughter. I promise to be fun for you.

NAME 1: I know I can trust you with everything I am. I promise to be trustworthy.

NAME 2: You are strong for me when I fall apart. I will be strong for you.

NAME 1: You are tender towards me. I promise to be tender towards you.

NAME 2: You are calm for me. I promise to be calm for you.

NAME 1: You are passionate about me. I promise to be passionate about you.

NAME 2: You are my friend, always. I promise to always be your friend.

BOTH: You are my Beloved. I am your Beloved.

Nancy M. McKay

______, I marry you this day, freely and joyfully joining my life with yours. Blessed by the Spirit, may the love of our tomorrows be as the love we share today—wondrous as the stars' light, strong as an oak, faithful as the sun's rising, enduring as the sea. Wherever we go, whatever life brings, I promise to do all in my power to live this love with you.

Ann. B. Day

No one has touched my life like you.
No one can compare with you,
No one has made my heart leap and my soul dance,
nor set my mind alight with joy.
In your presence I have found my rest, my home, my self.
In your arms I have known such peace.
Today I give myself to you.
I am yours and ever shall it be.

Jonathan Blake

_____, in the presence of *(God/our friends/family)* I receive the gift of your love and offer you mine, as we are *(married/joined in civil union, etc.)* I promise to honor your individuality, even as I cherish our togetherness. I promise to be with you in joy and in struggle, even as I give you room to keep your own company. Grateful for your presence in my life, I will be attentive to our love, remembering the promises I have made this day.

Ann B. Day

On this momentous day,
it is my choice, my will, and my delight,
to wed you, my beloved.
Our love has changed my life; no more the search.
I have found you, my heart's desire,
and nothing will ever take me from your side,
You are my all and my only,
and with you shall I travel to my rest.

Jonathan Blake

I want to spend the rest of my life with you, only you.
I want to fall asleep each night with you by my side.
I want to tell you what fills my soul.
I want to love you for ever and for always.

I want you to be the parent of our child.
I want you to be my lifelong friend and lover.
I want you to awaken my life with your love.

I want us to fill the coming years with wonderful memories.
I want us to face everything together.
I want you. I want you and me. I want us.

Jonathan Blake

Statement of Intentions

_____ and _____, in each other's presence, you have found a home, a sanctuary where love is offered and trust is given and received. I invite you now to declare your intentions as you continue in your commitment to one another:

_____, you have chosen _____ to be your life partner.

Will you love and respect him/her? Will you be honest with him/her always?

Will you stand by him/her through whatever may come?

(Repeat with other person.)

And do you both promise to make the necessary adjustments in your personal lives in order that you may live in a harmonious and loving relationship together?

Laura Rose

I love you
I love you unconditionally
I will love you whatever tomorrow brings
I will love you however much you change
My love is like a rock upon which you can build your life
My love is constant, certain, and committed
My love will never waver, nor run dry
I declare that my lifelong vow
is to so love you, day by day and year by year
that I become your greatest blessing,
and your richest source of happiness.

Jonathan Blake

______ , I join my life with yours, believing that, together, we can learn love's lessons well. In you I have found a friend, a partner, a lover. And now you become my (wife/husband, spouse, etc.) As we (marry, join in union, etc.) in body and soul, I bring to you respect for the person you are, support for the person you are becoming, and hope for all our days ahead. In times of joy or sorrow, may our life be a sign of God's enduring love, a blessing to us and beyond us.

Ann. B. Day

You are so beautiful/handsome to me. You are my life, my light, my hope, my joy. You are my food, my drink, my music, and my song. You are my warmth, my shelter, my passion, and my rest. You are my world, and I am yours—your friend, your lover, and your soul mate. So let the whole world hear and know that I love you and I vow that my love will bring you joy.

Jonathan Blake

Vow for a Civil Union

Our ceremony was exceedingly simple—Lisa had a real thing about marriage as an institution, and sometimes I think if there hadn't been a puppy for her to pet at City Hall when we got our licenses we might never have done the civil union! It took a surprising amount of work to get this little bit written—but we had to find a common ground religiously (me being more Pagan, and wanting the "future lives" promise, and Lisa being, as she put it, a gardener and needing to think). Lisa also wanted to be sure that the vows acknowledged that we had already been together for more than twenty years, and that the ceremony wasn't perceived as the thing that made the relationship "real."

I, ______, take you, ______, for my partner in civil union. I offer you all that I have, all that I am, and all that I shall become. May we continue as we have begun, and, in all our lives, may we be reborn in the same time, and at the same place, that we may meet, and know, and remember, and love again.

Melissa Scott and Lisa Barnett

Vow for a couple together for years prior to a ceremony

______, as *(number of years together)* years ago,
I quietly joined my life with yours,
with God as our witness,
I do so happily today in this ceremony of *(marriage/civil union, etc.)*
before *(God/our family/friends, etc.)*.

With gratitude for what has been, and hope for what will be,
as your life partner and legally wedded spouse,
I promise to continue to love and respect you,
to support you, and to learn with you
the deepening lessons of trust, forgiveness, and joy
in the covenant of marriage—
in sickness and in health, in plenty and in want, in joy and in sorrow.
I make this promise with true intention to keep it

for as long as we both shall live.
With God's grace, may we grow in love
for ourselves and each other, our family, and world.

Ann. B. Day

Declaration of Community Support

Minister: We have all heard the African proverb that it takes a village to raise a child. This proverb conveys the truth that we need a community to nurture our growth as human beings not only at the beginning of our lives, but also as we journey through the various stages of life. You are that village for _____ and _____. Your love, care, and support of them is an incredible gift—a gift you give them today by being here and a gift you will continue to give them as you commit to loving and caring for them as individuals and as a couple in the years to come. I invite those who are able to stand and to voice your support for _____ and _____.

Community Response: We stand with you today to witness your sacred vows of commitment to one another. In a world that is not always welcoming to same-gender unions, we honor and celebrate your (number of years) years of faithfulness to one another. We acknowledge that every relationship needs people who will offer love, prayer, and support at different points along life's journey. _____ and _____, by our presence here today, we want you to know you have our love, our support, and our prayers.

Laura Rose

Pledge of Support for Family and Friends

Having journeyed with _____ and _____ on their separate paths, and come to witness as their paths merge, will you, the family and friends of these wo/men, give of your love and bestow upon them your support, counsel, and the gift of listening? Will you be there for them when the days are hard? Will you party with them when times are good? Will you teach them your wisdom and learn from their example? If so, please say (with some enthusiasm), "We will!!"

Greg Morisse

BLESSINGS, RITUALS, AND THE SACRAMENT OF HOLY COMMUNION

A Prayer of Blessing

A blessing speaks a word to people on behalf of God
and to God on behalf of those being blessed.
It states a wish, a prayer. It declares a vision, and so creates the reality it speaks.

I do not have much I can give you as you celebrate your union.
But I can voice a hope and say a prayer.

So ______ and ______ , I offer you a blessing.
That is, I offer you my word of affirmation, of faith, of hope, and of love for you both.

I honor you, and I give voice to what I see in your relationship and your commitment to one another.

These things I pray for you:
Joy, that you may delight in one another;
Strength, that you may live up to your promise;
Hope, that you may live through the challenges and toward the vision;
Faith, that you may trust and experience the ultimate goodness of life;
and Love, that you may live fully and freely and unconditionally.

May God journey with you,
and may you journey with God
this day, and the next, and all the days to come.

Stephen Griffith

A Handfasting/Binding/Joining Ceremony

It is customary to wrap a white cloth or ribbons or some such around your joined hands and say one of the following:

That which God/Love has joined together, let no other seek to divide.
Or
Those whom God/Love hath joined together let no person put asunder.
Or
Your lives consist of colored threads, which are now forever to be woven together. Let the joining of these hands, and the binding of these wrists mark the beginning of the tapestry of your marriage. May your love be the golden thread that provides illumination and beauty to your days, and may your joy be the silver thread that reflects the light of the stars, your dreams come true in each other's safe embrace.
Or
Joined in heart, woven in soul, dancing in joy, moving to the rhythm of love, never to be apart, never to be separated; one destiny, one tapestry, one dream.

Jonathan Blake

Wedding Blessing

Loving God, pour out your Holy Spirit on _____ and _____ . Fill them with your passion for justice, love for all, and deep joy as we celebrate their marriage *(holy union, life commitment ceremony)*. Enable them to walk together with joy and gentleness as they seek to follow the footsteps of your son Jesus every day of their lives.

Ruah, Sophia, Life-giver, open the hearts of everyone assembled here and fill _____ and _____ with your blessings. Celebrate with us as we celebrate their marriage *(or other ceremony)*. Be with them in times of joy and times of tears and keep their love as vibrant and vital as it is today. We remember that their marriage *(or other ceremony)* is an act of faith and courage and pray that they will seek to do justice, to love mercy, and to walk humbly with you every day of their lives. Thank you for the gifts you bestow and the gifts we receive in and through this celebration of love. Amen.

Frances A. Bogle

An Exchange of Rings

(For a longtime couple exchanging rings they have previously worn as a sign of their commitment)

_____ , I give you again the ring you have worn
as a symbol of our commitment.
Wear it now, also,
as a symbol of our *(marriage /legal union, etc.)*.
As in days past, so to in days to come
may it remind you of my abiding love for you.

Ann B. Day

Community Laying On of Hands and Blessing

In the Christian tradition, the laying on of hands is a means for bestowing a blessing not only with words but with a tangible action that symbolizes the Light and Spirit of God resident and flowing in and through each of us and flowing out to those upon whom we desire to bestow blessing.

People move forward.

As we gather around _____ and _____ , we live out a beautiful prayer attributed to St. Teresa of Avila: "God has no body now but yours. No hands, no feet on earth but yours. Yours are the hands with which God reaches out to bless the world."

Let us pray: Gracious God, you created us to live in relationship and participate in the miracle of love. Today we unite our hearts and our hands in blessing _____ and _____ with strength, patience, and love so they have all they need to carry one another through each day and through whatever life brings. As the community that loves and supports this holy union and this beloved couple, give us the grace to fulfill our vow to be a tangible presence in their lives: carrying them in our hearts and prayers, offering practical assistance when needed, and walking beside them, as they make their way home today, and as they make their way on life's journey. We pray all these things in the spirit of the One who is the Source of all Love. Amen.

Laura Rose

A Benediction, as the Service Closes

You walked in here as one person, you leave as another. You walked in here as one couple, you leave as another. You are changed. You have joined the magic of covenant to the love you already had. May it continue to change you and may the uncaged God, the free spirit, the holy vows mark your goings out and your coming ins from this day forward, even forevermore. Amen.

Donna Schaper

Liturgy for Blessing by Friends and Family Using Symbols of Rings and Light

Before the ceremony

The couple's rings are placed atop two long candles outside the sanctuary door with a good friend guarding them. As guests arrive for the service, they are invited to bless the rings and candles. A small bowl of water and scattered flower petals are placed nearby, in case a guest wishes to use them in blessing.

During the ceremony

As part of the procession, the candles are brought forward and placed on either side of a third candle—a "unity" candle. The rings are removed after the vows by the officiant and exchanged with a description of how the rings and the relationship have been lovingly blessed by the circle of the couple's friends and family.

Unity Candle

______ and ______ have chosen to light a unity candle as a way of symbolizing their promises before God, and to one another.

If you look up the word "unity" in a dictionary, you will find it has a rich array of meanings:

the state of becoming one;

the quality of being in accord or harmony;

the quality of being one in spirit, mind, feeling;

becoming a whole;

constancy, continuity, and togetherness of purpose, action and goals . . .

And I would add a line from a very old poem that was popular in the 1960s: "it's standing together, and facing all that life brings from the same direction."

Parents/dear friends light the two tall candles and hand a lit candle to each partner.

As ______ and ______ light a single candle, the candle that signifies all these meanings of "unity," they do so from candles that you have blessed today.

May the light that blooms from the light each of them holds individually and that they bring together now. *Couple lights the unity candle.* Grow and grow in their hearts, in their lives, and in the world, from today forward, and evermore.

Sharyl B. Peterson

The Sharing of Wine Ceremony

You have shared together the fruits of love, and your times together have been blessed. Drink now this rich wine, fruit of the earth, symbol of life, of creation, of passion, and of love. *The couple sip wine from the same silver vessel.*

May the power of love as strong wine ever flow within your veins and may the taste of the grape ever remind you of this moment when your mouths, as your lives, were burning with the joy of each other.

Jonathan Blake

The Sharing of Honey Ceremony

You have tasted the sweetness of love, intense and profound. Refresh each other now with the touch of honey upon your lips. *The partners in turn collect a tiny amount of honey with a silver spoon from a silver vessel and give it to each other.*

May the touch of your lips, as your lives, be delicate and sweet and, as a thousand bees upon a thousand flowers have gathered this rich nectar, may the exercise of your love be as constant and as colorful all your days.

Jonathan Blake

A Prayer of Blessing over the Food

This feast is a sign of your reign, O God. It is a picture of the joy you intend for all people all of the time. Let us raise our glasses first to you and then to each other, and let us promise to live in the feast, now and always. Amen.

Donna Schaper

Communion Liturgy for Same-Gender Loving Marriage

Invitation (minister)

Jesus did his best work at parties; he loved to eat with his friends and followers—all of them, even those who later fled from him, betrayed him, denied him. On this day of celebration, as we bask in all that love can accomplish, it is a right and good thing that we share a meal together of bread and cup. As we approach Christ's table, we remember his love, his devotion, his sacrifice, and his victory. On this day, we also remember all the obstacles that have blocked our path; we acknowledge the spiritual work it took to get here. As we share these simple elements, we remember that Christ's ministry is an open door for us, an invitation to all of God's children to embrace the fullness of life in God, our Creator.

Prayer of Thanksgiving

God of all creation, Spirit of our living hope, fall afresh on this table. We remember your Passover covenant and we give you thanks for all our ancestors in faith. We rejoice that you teach us the way of reconciliation with you and all people everywhere. We give thanks that you remain faithful to your covenant even when we are faithless. Overwhelm these simple elements of bread and cup. Transform this ordinary ritual into holy food. Meet us here, O Christ, that we may be filled by your spirit and replenished by your grace. Amen.

Remembering the Story

(For two voices, perhaps the couple, perhaps those who have come as trusted attendants)

VOICE 1: On the night of betrayal and desertion . . .

VOICE 2: And on the morning after the resurrection . . .

VOICE 1: Jesus set a table for his disciples one last time, that they might strengthen one another in the face of certain trial and persecution.

VOICE 2: Jesus gathered his disciples on a beach, to celebrate the joyful wonder of the resurrection and the awesome power of God's love.

VOICE 1: In his words, Jesus sought to give the disciples a defiant hope that would sustain them through all the pain and doubt that would follow.

VOICE 2: In his words, Jesus sought to inspire the disciples to use the depth of their experiences—the joy and the struggles—to preach the good news of God's grace.

VOICE 1: He gathered them around a table. On this table was bread. Jesus lifted it up, he blessed it and broke it. As he did this he looked each of them in the eye and said: "This is my body. It is broken for you."

VOICE 2: "This is my body. It is broken for you."

VOICE 1: "Whenever you break bread together, remember me."

VOICE 2: And so it was, in the same way, Jesus took the cup.
He blessed it and said: "This is the cup of the new covenant of forgiveness and healing."

VOICE 1: "This is the cup of the new covenant, of forgiveness and healing."

VOICE 2: "When you drink it: remember me."

Blessing (minister)

At this table and on this beach, we re-member Jesus. We acknowledge the brokenness of the Body, and the brokenness in our lives, and we invite the Holy Spirit to transfigure us, to put us back together. In the breaking of the bread, we can experience wholeness. Jesus did not promise us always an easy life of banquets and parties. To follow Jesus is to risk the pain and agony of defeat and to believe that, even in defeat, God makes us new again. As we drink of his cup, Jesus reminds us that our sins are not permanent in the eyes of God and that neither among individuals nor nations need there be conflict and war. We testify in this sacrament to the power of love to sustain us in the days ahead.

Consecration

Gracious and Powerful God, Loving and Vulnerable God, you came to us as an infant child, trusting human protection. You came to us as a mighty prophet trusting human openness. You came to us as a Living Savior, trusting that we would follow. Send now your Holy Spirit to bless these simple elements, that they may be for us the sign and presence of Jesus Christ. Bless this table that all may be free to come to it. Bless every child and every parent, every friend and every enemy, that we may all be one. With Christ on our hearts, we pray. Amen.

Sharing the Elements

Post Communion Prayer

For all that you give us and all that beckons us toward, we give you thanks. For the daily bread you offer us and for sustaining us on the journey, we give you praise. For the unity that you create, we lift up your name: Jesus Christ our Head, Amen.

Greg Morisse

Holy Communion Concluding in Community Blessing of the Couple

Invitation to the Table

This is a table at which God says to each one gathered here: you are invited. No matter who you are or where you are on life's journey, you are welcome. So come and eat and drink around this table that the hungers of your soul may be filled.

Remembering the Story

Around this table of Holy Communion, we gather to remember the great hospitality of Jesus the Christ: friend of outcasts, healer of the sick, liberator of the poor, disturber of the peace—one with the courage to speak the truth that love commands and open doors of inclusion and welcome no matter the cost. We remember how Jesus gathered with his disciples on the night of the Passover meal on the eve of his arrest and death. He took the bread that they were about to share, and he gave thanks to God and broke it saying: This is my body, broken for you. As often as you eat this bread, do so in remembrance of me. In the same way after supper, he took the cup and, giving thanks, offered it to all of them saying: Drink of this, all of you, for this is my cup of the new covenant.

Blessing of the Bread and Cup

Come, Holy Spirit, transform these ordinary things, this grain and fruit of the vine, that as we share them they may be filled with your extraordinary presence. Come and mend and heal all that is broken in us. Come and weave together the threads of our lives that we might celebrate together the beauty of ______ and ______ 's union and the union of our lives on this day, at this table where there are no strangers, only friends.

These are the gifts of God, for the people of God.

Let us share the feast.

Sharing the Bread and Cup

Community Blessing *(Inviting the community to gather and lay hands on the couple)*

Divine Spirit, in whom we live and move and have our being, pour out grace on ______ and ______ that they may hear the sweetness of your melody and join in rhythms of your dance all the days of their lives. May your invisible hand continue to weave together their lives as they seek each day to live out the commitment they have made to one another.

Give each of them the strength and the patience to love each other well and to practice living generously with one another and all those who cross their paths. Grant to them a love that will sustain them in times of hardship and that will deepen over time and broaden through shared experiences. We thank you for the gift of love and the ability to open our hearts in tenderness. Bless each one gathered here today that we may each go from this place reminded of our love and responsibility for one another and for all of creation. Amen.

Laura Rose

Concluding Remarks and Charge

Well, you did it! We are witnesses today of this amazing commitment you have made to each other. But before we go off and party and you think it's all over, I want to say to you that now is really when the work begins. Planning a party is a piece of cake compared to carving out a life together that is joyful, productive, and honest. You know that, but I have to say it, so that we all remember it.

There will be and are enemies of your love. Some of them come from personal demons, enemies within each of you that can push the other away. Some of them come from this society where too many people still don't recognize your love for one another as legitimate. Some may even come from people who love you and are well-meaning, but do things to drive you apart.

Today I am going to give you a magic spell to conquer all those demons. They can all be killed by one thing: joy. The last thing I want to say today is that you need to laugh a lot, make love a lot, help other people to laugh a lot, dance a lot, write joyful things, sing joyful things, create beauty in your home and your work. Defy any darkness in the world, in your work or in your home, with abundant armfuls of joy. I can give you no greater gift than that, and it actually is not mine to give, but God's. For if you remember that the two of you are a part of a much greater love, you will find the power you need to shine always the way you shine today.

Rochelle A. Stackhouse

At the Time of the Album's Arrival

We are thankful, O God, for the smiles on each face and the love in each heart. We wonder why we had so few quiet moments—and we wonder how we could ever have looked so good. Ritualize the joy in us so that every year on our anniversary we go back to these pictures and rejoice. Ritualize our wedding joy so that we find a way to sneak feast into our ordinary ways of living. Manage our lives not by the fleeting joy of our big day but by the ongoing gladness we have in each other. Some people think nothing is a miracle and others know that everything is a miracle. Let us be a part of the last group, enchanted by and with life. Re-enchant us daily with each other and with life. Amen.

Donna Schaper

COMPLETE CEREMONIES

Wedding Ceremony

Because they wish to dedicate themselves to each other, and because they seek that joy that comes when two become joined in body, mind, and spirit, _____ and _____ come seeking the greater fulfillment of their lives in marriage. We are privileged to share the celebration of their dedication to one another.

Let us pray: Gracious God, In the quiet of this very special moment, we pause to give thanks for all the rich experiences of life that have made ______ and ______ the persons they are and have brought them to this high point in their lives. Our years are filled with new beginnings, and we are grateful for the twists and turns of personal history that bring these two to this day, prepared to explore a new era with zest and joy and hopefulness.

We are grateful, as well, that these two, who share values formed and tested on many occasions, are strengthened by what they find in one another. May their loving relationship grow and mature with each passing year until the latter days become even more wonderful than the first. In the spirit of all that is holy, we ask it. Amen.

______ and ______ , today, as you publicly declare your love for and your commitment to one another, you are setting forth on one of life's greatest adventures. Through your years together, you will discover and create your own unique definition of what it means to be a couple. You will find it exciting and wondrous, and frequently surprising. Whatever its final shape may be, it will be distinctly your very own.

We who share this occasion with you today want to give you, along with our best wishes, our blessing—that in good times and in bad, you will always feel the touch of the Eternal upon your lives; and wherever you may go, and whatever you may do, you will always and everywhere be with God.

______ and ______ , as you stand before these friends and witnesses, I charge you to remember that love and loyalty alone are the foundation for a happy and enduring home. If you keep the solemn vows that you are about to make, and if you seek to live by the very best that you know, your lives will be full of peace and joy, and the home you are establishing will abide through every change.

I charge you both, as well, to grow so that each gains your greatest satisfaction from giving peace and happiness to the other. Cherish the vision of your growing love. Let it be consecrated by sharing of common events. Believe in this commitment. It is binding. It is as close as we come to final truth in human relationships.

(Readings, if desired)

Now, ______ , I would like to ask you a question.
Do you take ______ to be your wedded partner, and, in the presence of these witnesses, do you promise you will do everything in your power to make your love for him/her a growing part of your life? Will you stand by her/him in sickness and in health; in poverty or in wealth, as long as you both shall live?
(Partner answers:) I will.
(Repeat for other partner.)

Meditation, if desired

Now, ______ , would you please take ______ 's hands in yours and repeat after me:
I, ______ , take you, ______ , to be my wedded partner; to love and to cherish from this day forward; in darkness and in light, with understanding and trust, to love and to stand beside, for all our days.
(Repeat for other partner)

What pledge do you offer that you will fulfill your vows? *(A ring)*

Bless, O God, these rings, symbolizing endless love, that each one who gives and each one who receives may abide in thy peace and continue in thy favor, through all their lives together. Amen.
This emblem of constancy and truth, I give you, ______ , to be the visible sign of your heart's fidelity. As you place this ring on ______ 's finger, repeat after me:
With this ring I thee wed, and pledge to thee my faithfulness.
(Repeat for other partner.)

Let us pray. May these two, ______ and ______ , be blessed with the gifts of joy, hope, and ever enlarging horizons. May they know peace—not of the silent pool, but of deep waters flowing. May the dreams we celebrate with them this day become the realities of tomorrow and tomorrow and tomorrow. May the vows that have here been made be consecrated in the earthy everydayness of their life together. And may the deep intimacies they share flow into and enrich the river of existence, until all who know them will learn something of Eternity because of who and what they are together. In the spirit of all that is holy we pray. Amen.

Forasmuch as _____ and _____ have consented together in wedlock, witnessed the same in the presence of these witnesses, pledged their faith and love to each other, and declared the same by joining hands, and by the giving and receiving of rings, I pronounce that they are a wedded couple.

May the faith that gives us freedom,
the hope that gives us courage
and the love that gives us life,
abide in your hearts always,
shedding light upon your lives and
transforming all your days. Amen.

_____ and _____ , you may now kiss one another.
It is my very great pleasure to introduce this newly married couple.
_____ and _____ .

G. Clyde Dodder

Simple Wedding Service

Greeting

Beloved, we gather in this place to celebrate and affirm the love that _____ and _____ share. Through this ceremony they will come together as a legally married couple, enjoying for the first time the legal affirmation of the relationship they have built for over *(length of their relationship before marriage)*. We are so glad you are here to celebrate with us!

Invitation

Throughout their lives _____ and _____ have been blessed by God's love and of the love of family and friends. Like the fish and the loaves, that love has multiplied when it was needed, feeding and sustaining them through the difficult times in their lives. God's love, the love and welcome of *(this church name or the denomination, where appropriate)*, and your love, have been the rich loam in which the roots of their relationship have grown deep and strong. As friends and family you have supported them, sustained them, laughed and cried with them, and held and carried them as they moved toward this day.

It is a joy to be with them as they celebrate their legal marriage today and as they affirm the love they share with *(include names of any children).*

Marriage is a legal and ecclesial event that asks the gathered community to recognize and bless a special relationship. Friends, ______ and ______ invite you to share with joy and wonder in this special occasion and ask for your blessing. Do you offer your blessing to them? If so, please say "We do."

Those assembled reply: We do.

Opening prayer

Ruah, spirit of life, more abundant than the grains of sand in the desert, greater than the highest mountains, green and growing like fields of grain, we thank you for the beauty and mystery of the earth and for the love we share in this community of faith.

We know you in the wind that sculpts the desert. You are molten lava birthing a new island. We feel you shaping the world, calling us to be cocreators with you.

When we open ourselves to your sacred presence, we experience you in the great blue heron preening in the sun. You dive with the brown pelican catching a fish, and rest on one leg with a snowy egret asleep in the sun. You fill our hearts with peace when we are distressed and weary. Help us remember that, in the difficult, scary times that happen in every relationship, your love is also with us.

You whisper in the brown grass of autumn and dance with the swirling leaves. You sing in the voices of frogs and crickets, sharing the joy and struggle of all of creation. You love us, even when we feel unlovable, and you call us to love each other with open hearts.

You are the voice of love and justice calling us into right relationship with you and all of creation. Be with us today as we bless ______ and ______, and all who seek to create new relationships rooted in your abundant love. Amen.

Celebrating the Ceremony

Marriage is a ceremony uniting two people in a special bond of commitment and love. When they began their relationship, ______ and ______ created a covenant of love. In the midst of oppression and fear, they believed in the promised new life that is ours through Christ. They believed in God's promise of eternal acceptance, and in each other's promises of love. Today's ceremony is a continuation of the covenant of love that has been the heart and soul of their relationship for so many years.

______ and ______ , it is time for you to turn to each other and reaffirm the deep and abiding love you share. You will also make new promises to each other and with *(names of any children)* who are blessed to share this new season of your life together.

Reaffirmation of Love

______ , I ask you to reaffirm you love for ______ :

One partner says: ______ , through this ceremony of marriage I reaffirm my deep and abiding love for you. You are the one who cares for me and comforts me, who shares my hopes and dreams, who knows my deepest fears and wounds and shares my journey toward healing. You have been and continue to be my greatest supporter, believing in me even when others don't and I doubt myself. You help me laugh, and remind me that tears are a blessing. Together we celebrate the wonders of love that knows no bounds. With you I experience God's presence in miraculous ways. Today, I reaffirm and celebrate you, and our relationship.

(Repeat with other partner)

Rededication of Lives

______ , I ask you to turn to ______ and rededicate your life and love to her/him:

One partner says: ______ , I rededicate my life and love to you. I promise to love you in my own way all of the days of our lives. I promise to support and encourage you, to challenge and invite you to be your best self every day. With the best of my ability and all of my humor and strength I promise to support and hold you in times of crises, to laugh and celebrate with you in times of joy. I am committed to staying in the struggle with you during the difficult times, and to dancing and

resting beside you in times of abundance. May the covenant we share continue to be a witness to the power and sacredness God's of love at work in the world. Will you continue to walk with me in the journey of faith?
Other partner replies: I will!
(Repeat with other partner.)

Blessing of Rings and Hands

Will you join hands?
Holy God, bless all of the circles of love that sustain and unite _____ and _____. Their rings *(include or omit)* selected long ago and worn with pride, are the visible symbols of the love that unites them. Bless these rings and the courage it takes to wear them. Bless their hands so that they may hold each other with love and do your work of justice in the world. Bless them with abundant love, with family and friends who will support and care for them through all of seasons of their lives. May their love and courage strengthen and sustain us all. Amen.

Children's Pledge *(if appropriate)*

(Name of child/ren), you are an incredible part of _____ and _____ 's life together. You experience their love every day and share your love with them. Do you promise to share your love with them every day and the help them as much as you can to make your family a place of hope and love? If so say "I/We do."
Reply: I/We do!

By the power of _____ *(a state, a denomination)* and Almighty God, we now pronounce you (legally) married. You may share a kiss!

Benediction and Sending Forth

Now, justice seekers, people of courage, lovers of all, may God bless you and keep you, protect you and challenge you as we go forth to share the power and hope of abundant love with the world! Amen.

Frances A. Bogle and Deborah L. Clark

Ceremony for Signing the Certificate

(when a church service happens later or as a free-standing occasion)

Words of Welcome

Friends, we have gathered here to celebrate and to bear witness to the legal marriage of _____ and _____ . We know the love that brought them together *(number of)* years ago, is sacred, and is a gift of God. Today, we share this moment of celebration and recognition with an ever wider number of people. Today, we recognize, with church and with state, that all of God's children are created equal, that there is no second class when it comes to truly and deeply loving relationships and families.

As most of you know, _____ and _____ will have a wedding ceremony and reception at a later time. But they couldn't wait to sign the license and make this dream a reality! So we come here together, assured of God's blessing, assured of the *(name of state's)* affirmation to do just that—to declare with loving couples and families throughout the state, that far from being legal strangers, they are legally wed to one another from this day forward.

God especially knows that when we look forward to a new and better future, as we do today, we also look back to what brought us to this place. We look back to those pioneers of our faith, those pioneers of justice who made this day possible. We recall days from very recent memory when _____ and _____ could not hope, could not even dream of this day coming. We recall days of chanting and holding signs on the statehouse steps. We recall countless e-mails, petitions, and meetings with lawyers, teachers, advocates, and congregations. And we remember this day how much work is yet to be done, in this state and beyond. We commit ourselves to this ongoing work, even as today we celebrate its fruits. _____ and _____ , how fitting it is that you two should take one of the first bites!

Prayer of Invocation

God of history and hope, God whose Spirit wells up in our giddy laughter and in our tears, God of equality and compassion, praise be to you this day. Move within our hearts and spirits. Be present at the core our souls. Let your truth, love, and beauty punctuate the end of these covenant sentences, not only with the comma of new revelation, the period of justice served, but also the exclamation of joy! Let us rejoice and celebrate! Amen.

The Questions

Understanding that marriage is an occasion that brings our minds and hearts to the very idea of loving families, and one that touches many lives, we recognize that not everyone could be here today who would want to be. We lift up especially *(names of deceased)* and the other friends and family who could not be here for this celebration, but who are surely with us in spirit. For those of you who are here, however, I have some very important questions for you all. First and foremost . . .

_____ and _____ , do you want to get married? *Reply:* We do!

For children: _____ , do you want your mommies/daddies to be married? *Reply:* We do!

For family and guests: Do you who come here today promise to support and encourage these two in this commitment. *Reply:* We do!

Do you _____ , take _____ to be your lawfully wedded partner?
Reply: I do!
Repeat for other partner

Will you continue to share your joys and burdens? Will you be honest with one another and faithful to one another always, whatever the future may hold? *Reply:* We will!

Candle Lighting

God of our mothers and fathers, God of our children, God of our brothers and sisters, God of our chosen family, we light from these candles this single candle as a symbol of that divine spark of your love and joy that is present with us today.

Concluding Prayer

Holy God, let us sing out and celebrate. Today is a day for justice and a day for joy. Today is a day in which we are able to fully recognize, with an ever wider number of people, something that we have known for a long, long time . . . that love makes a family!

Until recently, many could not hope, could not dream of this day coming. Well . . . dreams we would not let ourselves dream, hopes we would not let ourselves hope, come true this day. When it comes to those dreams of equality and justice for all your children, we know that our dreams are your dreams, God. And today, _____ and _____ become living symbols of your dream come true, God!

May we take inspiration from their courage in the struggle for justice for same-sex couples; may we take inspiration from their courage to create and raise a family together, long before our state would even begin to recognize their love. We already know that their family is blessed. We already know that their love is sacred. We already know these things, but what a joy it is to be able to celebrate it this day, to give thanks, to say it loud and proud for all to hear! Continue to bless them with your presence, with your courage, with your ongoing possibilities for their lives and for the lives of those around them. May we all go forward inspired to make peace and justice a reality for all your children. Amen.

Signing of the Certificate

Declaration of Marriage

By the authority committed to me as an ordained minister, and the authority vested in me by the State of _____ , I declare that _____ and _____ are now fully and legally married. What we have joined together on yhis day, let no law or amendment or political ambition tear apart. What God has joined together, let no one put asunder.

Daniel A. Smith

WEDDING RITUAL

PROCESSION

(singers, drummers, participants, and bridal couple welcomed into gathered community)

Casting the circle *(Elements for the altar are already in place at each corner)*

PRAYER OF THE EAST *(lighting incense)*

Hail, Guardians of the Watchtowers of the East,
Powers of Air!

We invoke you and call you.
Rising Sun. Vast Skies. Clear minds.
By the air that is Her breath,
Fill our lungs with freshness,
Be here now!

PRAYER OF THE SOUTH *(lighting a candle)*

Hail, Guardians of the Watchtowers of the South,
Powers of Fire!
We invoke you and call you,
Flaming One! Summer's warmth. Spark of life.
By the fire that is Her spirit,
Send forth your flame,
Be here now!

PRAYER OF THE WEST *(bringing ocean water and sprinkling it)*

Hail, Guardians of the Watchtowers of the West,
Powers of Water!
We invoke you and call you,
Evening Star. Rainmaker. Pounding Surf.
By the waters of Her living womb,
Send forth your flow,
Be here now!

PRAYER OF THE NORTH *(bringing sand to the altar and sprinkling it)*

Hail, Guardians of the Watchtowers of the North,
Powers of Earth—Cornerstone of all Power!
We invoke you and call you,
Stone, Mountain, Field, Sand,
Come! By the earth that is Her body,
Send forth your strength,
Be here now!

PRAYER OF THE CASTING

The circle is cast. We are between the worlds.
Feel the Spirit within you. Greet the spirits near you.
We have now set this time and this space as sacred—

filled with Spirit and Love.
We are now all connected.
Blessed Be.

Making the sacred circle visible in our midst with the stones of our lives

(Invite people to put life—their memory and desire, their faith and hope and love, their spiritual intention—imaginatively into a stone by breathing deeply and sending their breath through their hands into the stone. These words may help:)

The bridal couple welcome to the circle the presence of loved ones, living and passed on, who are unable to be with us today. You may wish to do so as well. There are other possibilities: prayers for your own family; for the sick; for the oppressed; for those in any kind of trouble; for those who cannot pray; for imagination, surprise, and grace beyond our understanding and control.

(Instrumental music, singing, chanting or humming are helpful)

Please place the stones behind you, creating a circle.

Readings *(Suggestions "Touched by an Angel" by Maya Angelou, "In Love Made Visible," by May Swenson)*

Songs *(Suggestions "A Chloris" by Reynaldo Hahn, "Con El Viento," Anonymous, Spanish Renaissance)*

WEDDING CEREMONY

Introduction *(with improvisation in breath, sound, word, and movement)*

Everybody take a big breath, a deep sigh. Here we are.
Marriage. Call out words that come to you as you think of marriage. *(Assembly replies.)*

Marriage is: A way of life. A way into life. A way for life. The fullness of life. A shelter. A place of unconditional love, forgiveness, safety, nurture. A cauldron where challenges and opportunities, joy and sorrow, anger and delight, all the intensity and all the drudgery of an entire lifetime roil us round in a great stew, refining us, bringing out the best in us, making us tasty and resplendent, making us shine with the glory

of love fire-tried and purified. A gateway. Like no other on this earth for growth, happiness, and fulfillment. A great mystery.
(Add in any here from suggestions of those who have gathered.)

The end of _____ 's life as a single person. *(Add, if one or both partners are taking new last names:)* _____ *(old last name)* will be no more.

The end of _____ 's life as a single person. _____ *(old last name)* will be no more.

Today they lay down their lives in order to take them up again, the same and yet not at all the same. Today they give themselves freely and fully to a lifelong commitment whose full consequences they cannot now know. Today they embark on the adventure of their lives, in the universe of love, unfolding in our midst.

Here we are, touching the mystery. Blessed be.

Exchange of Promises and Vows

EXCHANGE OF COMMITMENT BETWEEN _____ AND _____ AND FAMILIES
(they all stand)

The vows _____ and _____ will make affect not just each of them, but also everyone around them. Their union is not just of two individuals but of two families in the midst of a far flung community. We ask now if _____ 's and _____ 's families will promise to come together as one, and support _____ and _____ as they build their life together. We also ask _____ and _____ to commit to their families to continue to grow in love, and support their families as they build their lives. And so now, will the families please respond with a rousing "We Will" to each question:

Families, will you support, celebrate, and witness _____ and _____ 's relationship?

We will.

Will you forgive, and ask for forgiveness, when there is hurt and misunderstanding?

We will.

Will you strive with them, your whole life long, as they strive together in mutuality and love, to make their dreams a reality?

We will.

_____ and _____, will you support and celebrate with your families who have loved you, cared for you, and let you go?

We will.

Will you forgive, and ask for forgiveness, when there is hurt and misunderstanding?

We will.

Will you strive, your whole life long, for deeper understanding, love, and mutuality with your families?

We will.

EXCHANGE OF COMMITMENT BETWEEN _____ AND _____ AND THEIR GATHERED COMMUNITY *(all stand)*

You are _____ and _____'s community, far flung, but near and dear to them. You have come from diverse parts of their lives, but you all have in common your relationship with each of them. You have been brought together today as one community and are asked to witness, support, and celebrate their commitment.

You who gather today, will you support, celebrate, and witness _____ and _____'s relationship?

We will.

Will you forgive, and ask for forgiveness, when there is hurt and misunderstanding?

We will.

Will you strive with them, your whole life long, as they strive together in mutuality and love, to make their dreams a reality?

We will.

_____ and _____, this is your community, which over the years has grown, and which will continue to evolve throughout your lives. Do you promise to support and celebrate with your community?

We will.

Will you forgive, and ask for forgiveness, when there is hurt and misunderstanding?

We will.

Will you be a source of love and strength to them?

We will.

EXCHANGE OF VOWS BETWEEN ______ AND ______

In the presence of Spirit, all of creation, and this community, I now ask ______ and ______ to take one another's hands and to vow their love in marriage to one another.
Individuals are encouraged to create a personal introduction to vows, perhaps touching on significant memories or cherishing a personality trait and then continue in parallel promises. What follows is a small portion of this model wedding ceremony.

I promise to give you the best of myself and to ask of you no more than you can give.

I promise to respect you as your own person and to realize that your interests, desires, and needs are no less important than my own.

I promise to share with you my time and my attention and to bring joy, strength, and imagination to our relationship.

I promise to keep myself open to you, to let you see through the window of my world into my innermost fears and feelings, secrets and dreams.

I promise to grow along with you, to be willing to face changes in order to keep our relationship alive and exciting.

I promise to love you in good times and in bad, with all I have to give and all I feel inside in the only way I know how: completely and forever.

Exchange of Rings

(Officiant blesses rings in altar water with words about ocean water, womb water, living water, and endless circle of faithful, life-giving love.)

(Partners, in turn): With this ring I thee wed, with my body I thee worship, and with all my worldly goods I thee endow.

Handfasting

(Officiant introduces with words about this ancient tradition, unarmed, disarmed, wholly vulnerable and free and wraps _____ and _____'s hands in a scarf or stole.)

What is joined here, in the presence and blessing of the Divine, let nothing and no one ever sever.

CIVIL BLESSING

(From the judges' decision in Goodridge vs. Department of Health, *written by Massachusetts Supreme Court Chief Justice Margaret H. Marshall.)*

Marriage is a vital social institution. The exclusive commitment of two individuals to each other nurtures love and mutual support; it brings stability to our society. For those who choose to marry, and for their children, marriage provides an abundance of legal, financial, and social benefits. In return it imposes weighty legal, financial, and social obligations . . . . Without question, civil marriage enhances the "welfare of the community." It is a "social institution of the highest importance." Marriage also bestows enormous private and social advantages on those who choose to marry. Civil marriage is at once a deeply personal commitment to another human being and a highly public celebration of the ideals of mutuality, companionship, intimacy, fidelity, and family. Because it fulfills yearnings for security, safe haven, and connection that express our common humanity, civil marriage is an esteemed institution, and the decision whether and whom to marry is among life's momentous acts of self-definition.

SACRED BLESSING

The love with which _____ and _____ have been blessed is not just for their own enjoyment and benefit, but for the enjoyment and benefit of their families, their community, their society, and all of creation. Having given themselves to one another, they now take on all the duties and responsibilities of marriage. And so we bless them, as they begin their life together.

_____ and _____ kneel by altar. All who wish are invited to come forward, laying hands of blessing on the couple, voicing blessings softly. Music is appropriate here. All return to their place in circle, and hold hands. _____ and _____ stand, in center.

_____ *(Use first and, if appropriate, new last name)*, you are newly created in this act of transformation, an act that will continue moment by moment for the rest of your life. May you become more fully yourself, in joy and hope, in love and peace, in grace and glory, with each passing day. May you shower earth and heaven with blessing in all that you are, and all that you do, this day, and forevermore.

Repeat for other partner

_____ and _____ *(new last name, if appropriate)*, you are no longer two, but one. And yet, still also two. You are enfolded in the mysterious communion of Divine Love, that same love that shines in the stars, and sings in the wind, and dances in the waves, and makes a home in human families; in the human heart, mind, and soul; in flesh and blood. May you enter this mystery more fully each day and each night, in good times and in bad, with joy and thanksgiving, for the rest of your lives. May your children bless you; may your friends stand by you; and may those in need find help and comfort in you. May you together shower earth and heaven with blessing in all that you are and all that you do, this day and forevermore. In the power of Spirit, on behalf of this gathered body, and by the authority vested in me by the Commonwealth of Massachusetts, *(or other state, as appropriate)* I now pronounce you fully, really, and legally married.

Kiss! Applause!

OPENING THE CIRCLE

Universe and Guardians of the East, South, West and North,
Powers of Air, Fire, Water, and Earth,
We thank you for joining in our circle for Light and Love.
We ask for your blessing as you depart. Hail and Farewell.

We stand firmly on the Earth, grounded in our spiritual communion, and reach our hands to the sky as invitation to us all to return to this place in our hearts as we send _____ and _____ forth with the strength of our love and wishes for their boundless joy together.

The circle is now open, but unbroken,
May the peace of the Spirit
Go in our hearts.
Merry meet, and merry part.
And merry meet again.
Blessed be.

Ellen Oak

BIRDSEED AND PETALS—SOME SCATTERED WORDS

by Maren Tirabassi

Midnight prayer before the wedding

(refers to John 2)

God, I want the weather to be perfect, the food delicious, the music romantic, our relatives well-behaved and our guests sober enough to drive home. I want to look wonderful and have the photographs to prove it. I want to be poised and remember my vows and everyone's names. I want old friends and new ones to mingle, and awkward feelings to evaporate in the first ten minutes. I can imagine every kind of catastrophe, including someone not understanding the "same-gender" part of the "loving" in our invitation. I have run out of time, temper, tact, and toothpaste and so, wonderful party-God, I put you in charge of miracles and ask only for a good night's sleep. Amen.

Words of welcome for friends unsure but willing to learn . . .

(verbal or printed in program)

We extend a special welcome to family members, childhood friends, and work colleagues who are new to a wedding/covenanting context in which the couple are two men/women. We know how easy it would have been for you to have made an excuse and sent a gift rather than risk coming to this celebration. We are so glad that you came. In fact, of all our guests, we are most deeply touched by your presence supporting us today.

We assure you: your orientation is not going to stand out. You won't hear political speeches or be held responsible for intolerances of the past. You are not going to stare offensively at the benediction kiss or couples dancing. You are not going to say something stupid (at least not until after a few toasts). You are going to be moved by our ceremony and have a great time at our party. Our love for one another and for you is so deep it will absorb any awkwardness, and a blessing will rest on your own needs for tenderness, commitment to relationship, and willingness to be open to all God's children.

Prayer for uniting of faith and ethnic traditions

God, remind us not to lose ourselves in a one-issue wedding/covenant. We are focused on our sexual orientation and that is wonderful, but the political and cultural energy and excitement around this occasion threatens to erase the richness of our unique backgrounds. Help us to celebrate our *(ethnic or religious)* heritage, blending language and legacy of the past while letting go any parts of these traditions that we have experienced as critical or condemning. Remind us that our relatives' opinions are only relative. Help us to be balanced and creative as we honor our diversity and find new translations that support and enhance the commitment we make to one another. Amen.

Prayer for focus on one relationship in the midst of a large event

(such as City Hall steps after a new law takes effect!)
(Refers to 1 Kings 19 and Luke 15)

Gracious God, in the midst of the winds of cultural change, political earthquakes, and the bright fire of our celebration of marriage equality, we ask for your still small voice of blessing on _____ and _____, as they look into one another's eyes and pledge love and loyalty for this day and all their years of personal sickness and health, plenty and want, joys and sorrows. What these two people vow is as valuable as all the laws of the land. You who praised the seeking of a single lost sheep, coin, or wandering child, wrap the holy privacy of the joy of heaven and earth around these two, _____ and _____, about to be wed. Amen.

Prayer of exclusion, inclusion, and forgiveness

(Refers to Matthew 25)

Gracious and Holy God, secure in the covenant you have made in our hearts, we place these decisions in the light of your love, remembering that you told a parable about the inclusion and exclusion of those who expected to attend a wedding.

There are people who are part of our families or past histories *(name them, if desired)* whom we choose not to invite to the celebration of our wedding/union because their opinions damage the sacredness of this occasion. We pray that in years to come there may be healing and reconciliation that seem like a miracle now. We make this choice not in anger but in wisdom. We mourn their absence and the absence of *(their children, spouses)*, those who will not be present because of their attitudes.

There are people *(name them, if desired)* whom we are including even though they may not accept the invitation to our wedding/union. We are saddened by their hesitation in love but wish to offer them this responsibility. We will rejoice in their presence, respect their absence, and trust their courtesy.

Precious Savior and only Judge of us all, we offer our forgiveness of people, churches, schools, groups *(name them, if desired)* from whom we have experienced intolerance, cruelty, or abuse. What they have said and done is not acceptable, but we release ourselves from their continuing power for hurt and harm in our lives. We go forward unencumbered by the burden of hate they now must carry alone, until such a time as they may relinquish it to your grace and conversion. So lightened, we rejoice and return to the holy banquet that is the planning of our wedding/union. Amen.

Prayer after the rehearsal in a special place or for a special person

Sometimes a couple wants to honor a place special to their personal history or an influential person in their lives who has died. Bring a photograph if possible and a single flower or ribbon and take a private moment for prayer in these words or your own.

Spirit of hope and grace, on this lovely evening, we remember *(place or person)* and acknowledge that tomorrow's celebration would have never happened without this blessing in our lives. We remember . . . *(personalize)*

We dedicate this flower/ribbon that will be on the altar/in a bouquet tomorrow as a reminder for our eyes and hearts only of the importance of *(place or person)*. What is sad to us only makes us more compassionate toward others; what is special to us only makes us more aware of the daily miracles of life; what is remembered now teaches us to go forward tomorrow to make new and wonderful memories. Amen.

Wedding eve blessing for a Christian couple when the ceremony will be a civil one

(with hand alternating on the couple's heads or placed on their joined or handfasted hands)

May you be set as a seal upon one another's hearts,
for love is a strong as death and passion fierce as the grave.
Many waters cannot quench love,
neither can floods drown it. (Song of Solomon 7:6–7)

God, bless ______ and ______ on the eve of their wedding. May their vows be sacred and true and their kissing lips holy. May there be angel wings above the wedding attendants and may all their friends and family drink deeply the chalice of love. *(Holding the rings)*: As each of these rings is given and received, and in all the days to come, may there be your protective circle around ______ and ______ 's fingers, their loves, and their lives. Amen.

Prayer for anxious clergy on a first time celebrating a same-gender loving ceremony . . . or, "God, help this old dog learn to be a new wineskin!"

God, bless my words, my hands, and my advice (and my sanctuary) on the occasion of this first marriage of a same-gender loving couple. Help me to be honest with the tangle of my motivations so that I can help ______ and ______ be honest with theirs. Give grace to the liturgy of love we shape together. Help me to protect them from hurtful comments by members of the congregation. Help me care for the congregation and let down my defensiveness enough to hear genuine questions and opportunities to open hearts and minds. Forgive me all the times I will goof, and forgive me the pride that wants my performance to be perfect. Guide me as I help ______ and ______ relate to family and friends, understand marriage as far more than a bundle of benefits that has been too long withheld, and plan a great party! Amen.

Prayer for those who choose not to get married

(Refers to Genesis 1)

God, we celebrate ______ and ______ 's love and give thanks for their shared *(state number of)* years together. For one another they have been *(personalize: handball competitors, caregivers, partners in home and work, parents of ______ , confidants, etc.)*. We rejoice in their relationship. Contemporary marriage is not a model they admire or desire, even though it is now possible. Bless their decision to continue with the life of mutuality and tenderness they have fashioned in their community of support and in your eyes. May it be that—in the evening and the morning of every ordinary day and in the evening and morning of their last days—they truly echo your creative blessing, "This is good." Amen.

NOTES

INTRODUCTION

1. Dustin Lance Black, accepting an Academy Award for Best Original Screenplay, February 22, 2009.

CHAPTER ONE

1. Marvin Ellison, *Same-sex Marriage: A Christian Ethical Analysis* (Cleveland: Pilgrim Press, 2004), 11–12.
2. Evan Wolfson, interviewed in *Marriage—Just a Piece of Paper?* Katherine Anderson, Don Browning, and Brian Boyer, eds. (Chicago: University of Chicago Press, 2002), 349.
3. Edmund Leach, "The Social Anthropology of Marriage and Mating," in *Mating and Marriage*, Biosocial Society Series, no. 3, Vernon Reynolds and Kellett John, eds. (Oxford University Press, 1991), 93.
4. Stephanie Coontz, *Marriage, A History: How Love Conquered Marriage* (New York: Penguin, 2005), 2.
5. Ibid., 4.
6. Ibid., 5.
7. Mary Pipher, *Another Country: Navigating the Emotional Terrain of Our Elders* (New York: Riverhead Books, 1999).
8. Brian Grant, *The Social Structure of Christian Families* (St. Louis: Chalice Press, 2000), 72.
9. Andrew Chertin, *Public and Private Families: An Introduction*, 5th ed. (New York: McGraw Hill, 2008), 45.
10. Coontz, *Marriage*, 31.
11. Ibid., 32.
12. Wilma A. Dunaway, *The African-American Family in Slavery and Emancipation* (Cambridge University Press, 2003).
13. Chertin, *Public and Private Families*, 48.
14. Ellison, *Same-sex Marriage*, 14.
15. Virginia Ramey Mollenkott, *Omnigender: A Trans-religious Approach* (Cleveland: Pilgrim Press, 2001), 1.
16. Ellison, *Same-sex Marriage*, 18.
17. Rosemary Radford Ruether, *Christianity and the Making of the Modern Family: Ruling Ideology and Diverse Realities* (Boston: Beacon, 2000), 103.
18. Ellison, *Same-sex Marriage*, 15, quoting Boston's Gay & Lesbian Advocates & Defenders, "Equal Marriage from Five Angles."

19. Marvin Ellison and Judith Plaskow, *Heterosexism in Contemporary World Religion: Problem and Prospect* (Cleveland: Pilgrim Press, 2007), 7.
20. Joan Laird and Robert-Jay Green, *Lesbians and Gays in Couples and Families: A Handbook for Therapists* (San Francisco: Jossey-Bass, 1996), xii.

CHAPTER TWO

1. Douglas Stone, Bruce Patton, Sheila Heen, and Roger Fisher, *Difficult Conversations: How to Discuss What Matters Most* (New York: Penguin Books, 1999).
2. John Boswell, *Christianity, Social Tolerance, and Homosexuality* (Chicago: University of Chicago Press, 1980), 7.
3. Peter Gomes, *The Good Book: Reading the Bible with Mind and Heart* (New York: William Morrow, 1996), 9.
4. Rev. Richard A. Hunter, United Methodist pastor, quoted in "Our Mutual Joy," *Newsweek*, December 16, 2008.
5. Ronald E. Long, "Disarming Biblically Based Gay-Bashing," in *The Queer Bible Commentary*, ed. Deryn Guest, Robert Goss, Mona West, and Thomas Bohache (London: SCM Press, 2006), 1.
6. Leanne McCall Tigert, *Coming Out through Fire: Surviving the Trauma of Homophobia* (Cleveland: Pilgrim Press, 1999), 61.
7. James B. Nelson, *Humanly Speaking: A Foundation Paper on Human Identity, Relationships, and Sexuality* (Cleveland: United Church Board for Homeland Ministries, 1995), 31.
8. Kathleen Ritter and Anthony Terndrup, *Handbook of Affirmative Psychotherapy with Lesbians and Gay Men* (New York: Guilford Press, 2002), 37.
9. Virginia Ramey Mollenkott, *Sensuous Spirituality: Out from Fundamentalism*, revised and expanded (Cleveland: Pilgrim Press, 2007), 231–33.
10. Rosemary Radford Ruether, *Christianity and the Making of the Modern Family* (Boston: Beacon, 2000), 6.
11. David G. Myers and Letha Dawson Scanzoni, *What God Has Joined Together: A Christian Case for Gay Marriage* (New York: HarperCollins, 2005), 95.
12. Nelson, *Humanly Speaking*, 15.
13. Mona Guest, "Ruth," in *The Queer Bible Commentary*, 191.
14. Ken Stone, "1 and 2 Samuel," in *The Queer Bible Commentary*, 206.
15. Theodore W. Jennings, *The Man Jesus Loved: Homoerotic Narratives from the New Testament* (Cleveland: Pilgrim Press, 2003), 34.
16. Christopher King, "Song of Songs," in *The Queer Bible Commentary*, 356.
17. Jennings, *The Man Jesus Loved*, 234.
18. Walter Wink, "Biblical Perspectives on Homosexuality," *The Christian Century*, November 7, 1979.

CHAPTER THREE

1. Stephanie Coontz, *Marriage, A History: How Love Conquered Marriage* (New York: Penguin, 2005), 308.

2. Rev. Dr. Martin Luther King, speech commemorating the tenth anniversary of the Southern Christian Leadership Conference, August 16, 1967.

3. "Status of Same-sex Marriage," Wikipedia.

4. Human Rights Campaign, www.hrc.org.

5. Freedom to Marry, www.freedomtomarry.org.

6 Irvashi Vaid, *Virtual Equality: The Mainstreaming of Gay and Lesbian Liberation* (New York: Anchor Books, 1996), 30.

7. Laurie Israel, "Marriage, the Final Frontier: Learning from Each Other about Marriage," www.laurieisreal.com.

8. Susan Stewart, *Brave New Stepfamilies: Diverse Paths toward Stepfamily Living* (Thousand Oaks, Calif.: Sage Publications, 2007), 4.

9. Janet R. Jakobsen and Ann Pellegrini, *Love the Sin: Sexual Regulation and the Limits of Religious Tolerance* (New York: New York University Press, 2003), 5.

CHAPTER FOUR

1. This prayer was written by the Rev. Dr. Kenneth Orth and published in *Covenant Conversations: Pre-Marriage or Blessing Preparations with Same-Gender Couples* (Cleveland: UCC Coalition Publishers, 2007), 7.

2. Herbert Anderson and Robert Fite, *Becoming Married* (Louisville: Westminster John Knox Press, 1993), 87.

3. Ibid., 87.

4. Gretchen A. Stiers, *From This Day Forward: Commitment, Marriage, and Family in Lesbian and Gay Relationships* (New York: St Martin's, 2000), 82.

5. Monica McGoldrick and Kenneth V. Hardy, *Revisioning Family Therapy: Race, Culture, and Gender in Clinical Practice*, 2nd ed. (New York: Guilford Press, 2008).

6. Stiers, *From This Day Forward*, 89.

7. Paul W. Pruyser, *The Minister as Diagnostician* (Philadelphia: Westminster Press, 1976).

CHAPTER FIVE

1. Donna Schaper, "Invitation to Write Your Service," private papers.

CHAPTER SEVEN

1. William Stacey Johnson, *A Time to Embrace: Same-Gender Relationships in Religion, Law, and Politics* (Cambridge, Mass.: Wm. B. Eerdmans, 2006), 69.

2. Joretta Marshall, "Pastoral Care with Congregations in Social Stress," in *Pastoral Care and Social Conflict*, ed. Pamela D. Coutur and Rodney J. Hunter (Nashville: Abingdon Press, 1995), 173–74.

3. Charles Gerkin, *Prophetic Pastoral Practice: A Christian Vision of Life Together* (Nashville: Abingdon Press, 1991), 116–42.

CHAPTER EIGHT

1. Rene Girard and Yvonne Freccero, *The Scapegoat* (Baltimore: John Hopkins University Press, 1986).

2. Joretta Marshall, "Pastoral Care with Congregations in Social Stress, in *Pastoral Care and Social Conflict*, ed. Pamela D. Coutur and Rodney J. Hunter (Nashville: Abingdon Press, 1995), 176.

3. Larry Kent Graham, *Discovering Images of God: Narratives of Care among Gays and Lesbians* (Louisville: Westminster John Knox Press, 1997), 129.

4. Leanne McCall Tigert, *Coming Out through Fire: Surviving the Trauma of Homophobia* (Cleveland: Pilgrim Press, 1999), 134–35.

5. James Poling, *Deliver Us from Evil: Resisting Racial and Gender Oppression* (Minneapolis: Augsburg Fortress Press, 1996), 175–78.

6. Walter Wink, *The Powers That Be: Theology for a New Millennium* (New York: Doubleday, 1998), 34–36.

7. Rev. Gary M. Schulte, statement to the New Hampshire Senate Judiciary Committee, April 15, 2009.

8. Religious Institute on Sexual Morality, Justice, and Healing, 304 Main Avenue, 335, Norwalk, CT 06851, declaration available at http://www.religious institute.org/religious-declaration-on-sexual-morality-justice-and-healing.

CHAPTER NINE

1. Peter Barbosa, "Covenant Conversations," UCC Coalition, 31.

2. Kathryn M. Schreiber, personal papers.

CHAPTER TWELVE

1. Howard Moody, from *A Voice in the Village: A Journey of a Pastor and a People* (Bloomington, Ind.: Xlibris, 2009), 406.

2. Marie Harris, from *Weasel in the Turkey Pen* (New York: Hanging Loose Press, 1993), 57.

3. Some of Bishop Jon Blake's liturgical writings also appear in *Courage to Love—Liturgies for the Lesbian, Gay, Bisexual, and Transgender Community*, ed. Geoffrey Duncan (Cleveland: Pilgrim Press, 2002).

RECOMMENDED RESOURCES

BOOKS

Boswell, John. *Same-Sex Unions in PreModern Europe.* New York: Random House, 1994.

Cherry, Kittredge, and Zalmon Sherwood, eds. *Equal Rites: Lesbian and Gay Worship, Ceremonies, and Celebrations.* Louisville: Westminster John Knox Press, 1995.

Duncan, Geoffrey, ed. *Courage to Love: Liturgies for the Lesbian, Gay, Bisexual, and Transgender Community.* Cleveland: Pilgrim Press, 2002.

Ellison, Marvin M. *Same-sex Marriage: A Christian Ethical Response.* Cleveland: Pilgrim Press, 2004.

Ellison, Marvin M., and Judith Plaskow, eds. *Heterosexism in Contemporary World Religion.* Cleveland: Pilgrim Press, 2007.

Evan, Dina Bachelor. *Break Up or Break Through: A Spiritual Guide to Richer Gay and Lesbian Relationships.* Boston: Alyson Press, 2001.

Garner, Abigail. *Families Like Mine: Children of Gay Parents Tell It Like It Is.* New York: HarperCollins, 2004.

Guest, Deryn, Robert Goss, Mona West, and Thomas Bohache, eds. *The Queer Bible Commentary.* London: SCM Press, 2006.

Johnson, William Stacey. *A Time to Embrace: Same-Gender Relationships in Religion, Law, and Politics.* Cambridge: Eerdmans, 2006.

Kuntz, David J., and Bernard S. Schlager. *Ministry among God's Queer Folk: LGBT Pastoral Care.* Cleveland: Pilgrim Press, 2006.

Miner, Jeff, and John Tyler Connoley. *The Children Are Free: Reexamining the Biblical Evidence on Same-Sex Relationships.* Indianapolis: Jesus Metropolitan Community Church, 2002).

Robinson, V. Gene. *In the Eye of the Storm: Swept to the Center by God.* New York: Seabury Books, 2008.

Stiers, Gretchen A. *From This Day Forward: Commitment, Marriage, and Family in Lesbian and Gay Relationships.* New York: St Martin's Griffin, 2000.

Tigert, Leanne McCall, and Maren C. Tirabassi. *Transgendering Faith: Identity, Sexuality, and Spirituality.* Cleveland: Pilgrim Press, 2004.

ORGANIZATIONS/WEB SITES

Freedom to Marry (http://www.freedomtomarry.org/).

Gay and Lesbian Advocates and Defenders (GLAD) (http://www.glad.org/).

Human Rights Campaign (http://www.hrc.org/index.htm).

Institute for Welcoming Resources: National Gay and Lesbian Task Force (http://www.welcomingresources.org/).

Lambda Legal Defense and Education Fund (http://www.lambdalegal.org/).

Religious Institute on Sexual Morality, Justice, and Healing (http://www.religiousinstitute.org/).

The Center for Lesbian and Gay Studies in Religion and Ministry: Pacific School of Religion (http://www.clgs.org/).

DENOMINATIONAL ORGANIZATIONS

(Most denominations have an advocacy/resource organization. These are a few examples.)

American Baptists Concerned (http://www.rainbowbaptists.org/abconcerned.htm).

Affirmation: United Methodists for Lesbian, Gay, Bisexual, and Transgender Concerns (http://umaffirm.org/).

Dignity USA (Catholic) (http://www.dignityusa.org/).

Gay, Lesbian, and Affirming Disciples Alliance, Inc. (http://www.gladalliance.org/).

Integrity USA (Episcopalian) (http://www.integrityusa.org/).

Lutherans Concerned/North America (http://www.lcna.org/).

Metropolitan Community Churches (http://mccchurch.org/AM/Template.cfm?Section=Home).

More Light Presbyterians (http://www.mlp.org/).

The United Church of Christ Coalition for LGBT Concerns (http://www.ucccoalition.org/).

Unitarian Universalists Office of Bisexual, Gay, Lesbian, and Transgender Concerns (http://www.uua.org/aboutus/professionalstaff/identity-based ministries/bisexualgay/index.php).

INDEX OF CONTRIBUTORS

TOPICAL INDEX